ARMORED
FIGHTING VEHICLES
of World Wars I and II

ARMORED
FIGHTING VEHICLES
of World Wars I and II

Features 90 landmark vehicles from 1900–1945 with over 370 archive photographs

Armored cars, armored personnel carriers and self-propelled artillery, including the Gun Carrier, Jeep, Sturmmörser Tiger Assault Rocket Mortar, and many more

Jack Livesey

southwater

This edition is published by Southwater, an imprint of Anness Publishing Ltd
Hermes House, 88–89 Blackfriars Road, London SE1 8HA
tel. 020 7401 2077; fax 020 7633 9499
www.southwaterbooks.com; www.annesspublishing.com

Anness Publishing has a new picture agency outlet for images for publishing, promotions or advertising.
Please visit our website www.practicalpictures.com for more information.

UK agent: The Manning Partnership Ltd; tel. 01225 478444; fax 01225 478440; sales@manning-partnership.co.uk
UK distributor: Book Trade Services; tel. 0116 2759086; fax 0116 2759090;
uksales@booktradeservices.com; exportsales@booktradeservices.com
North American agent/distributor: National Book Network; tel. 301 459 3366; fax 301 429 5746; www.nbnbooks.com
Australian agent/distributor: Pan Macmillan Australia; tel. 1300 135 113; fax 1300 135 103; customer.service@macmillan.com.au
New Zealand agent/distributor: David Bateman Ltd; tel. (09) 415 7664; fax (09) 415 8892

Publisher: Joanna Lorenz
Senior Managing Editor: Conor Kilgallon
Senior Editor: Felicity Forster
Copy Editor and Indexer: Tim Ellerby
Cover Design: Balley Design Associates
Designer: Design Principals
Editorial Reader: Jay Thundercliffe
Production Manager: Steve Lang

ETHICAL TRADING POLICY

At Anness Publishing we believe that business should be conducted in an ethical and ecologically sustainable way, with respect for the environment and a proper regard to the replacement of the natural resources we employ.
As a publisher, we use a lot of wood pulp to make high-quality paper for printing, and that wood commonly comes from spruce trees.
We are therefore currently growing more than 750,000 trees in three Scottish forest plantations: Berrymoss (130 hectares/320 acres), West Touxhill (125 hectares/305 acres) and Deveron Forest (75 hectares/185 acres). The forests we manage contain more than 3.5 times the number of trees employed each year in making paper for the books we manufacture.
Because of this ongoing ecological investment programme, you, as our customer, can have the pleasure and reassurance of knowing that a tree is being cultivated on your behalf to naturally replace the materials used to make the book you are holding.
Our forestry programme is run in accordance with the UK Woodland Assurance Scheme (UKWAS) and will be certified by the internationally recognized Forest Stewardship Council (FSC). The FSC is a non-government organization dedicated to promoting responsible management of the world's forests. Certification ensures forests are managed in an environmentally sustainable and socially responsible way. For further information about this scheme, go to www.annesspublishing.com/trees

Previously published as part of a larger volume, *The World Encyclopedia of Armoured Fighting Vehicles*

NOTE
The nationality of each vehicle is identified in the relevant specification
box by the national flag that was current at the time of the vehicle's use.

PAGE 1: **Austin Armoured Car.** PAGE 2: **Beaverette Mk I and II Light Reconnaissance Cars.**
PAGE 3: **German StuG III Self-Propelled Gun.** PAGE 5: **Sd Kfz 251 Ausf A Medium Half-Track.**

PUBLISHER'S NOTE
Although the advice and information in this book are believed to be accurate and true at the time of going to press, neither the
authors nor the publisher can accept any legal responsibility or liability for any errors or omissions that may be made.

Contents

Introduction

During World Wars I and II, Armoured Fighting Vehicles (AFVs) developed to form one of the most complex groups of machines found on the battlefield. Excluding the tank, the AFV was represented by a wide and diverse range of machines that were both multi-tasking and multi-functional. They developed to form the core of the armoured division and were more numerous than the tank, even replacing the tank in some roles.

Before the invention of the internal combustion engine, people had tried to devise various ways of using wagons as crude mobile fighting platforms. Some of these contraptions were moderately successful, but the majority were ill-conceived. After 1900, AFV utilization began to increase, and development started to move quickly, establishing three main types of vehicle. The armoured car was the first of the AFVs to be deployed by the armed forces, with the Self-Propelled Gun (SPG) and the Armoured Personnel Carrier (APC) following on more slowly.

One of the most significant choices associated with AFV development related to the selection of wheels, tracks or a combination of both as the form of mobility. Early wheeled vehicles had very poor cross-country ability compared to that of the tank. This was particularly significant during World War I on the Western Front, where trench warfare and intense artillery bombardments made the battlefield unsuitable for armoured cars to operate. The SPG of this period was usually mounted on a tracked or semi-tracked chassis, however a

TOP: **The Gun Carrier was the first tracked self-propelled gun to go into service. Note the exposed position of the gun crew and the ammunition stored in the gap between the front cabin and rear engine compartment.** ABOVE: **Saloon car converted by the British Home Guard into an armoured fighting vehicle by fitting armour to the windows and radiator.**

small number of wheeled SPGs were developed. The APC started life as a battlefield taxi for the infantry, the very first being based on a tank design. Subsequently, vehicles were developed with a combination of wheels and tracks, known as "half-tracks". Being such useful and versatile vehicles, APCs were very quickly adapted into other roles, such as command vehicles, armoured ambulances and supply vehicles.

The armoured car quickly replaced horse-mounted cavalry in the role of battlefield reconnaissance. To fulfil this role it needed to be well armed and armoured, and capable of travelling at relatively high speeds. The main work of this

vehicle was to serve as the eyes of the army well in advance of its own front line. It had to rely on speed and agility to get out of trouble if observed by opposing forces. As the destructive power of anti-tank guns increased, armoured cars became much larger, surrendering speed for increased crew protection, with some examples mounting redundant tank guns and turrets.

The APC also underwent significant change during World Wars I and II, as new tactics were developed. Starting life as a crude tank conversion, the APC was quickly transformed into an open-topped vehicle for transporting infantry to the edge of the fighting zone, from where they were able to provide machine-gun support for the attacking infantry.

The SPG was initially developed in World War I to overcome the difficulty of moving artillery across heavily broken-up ground in order to keep pace with an advance or breakthrough. This role developed more generally into providing tank attacks with mobile artillery support capable of firing high-explosive rounds. This was particularly important because early tanks did not mount guns with a long enough range to fire a high-explosive round. SPGs of this period nearly always mounted their main ordnance in an open box on the top of a tracked vehicle, leaving the gun crew very exposed.

This book contains a wide range of AFVs from around the world, dating from the beginning of the 20th century to the end of World War II. The selection of machines concentrates on those that are of developmental interest or importance and which demonstrate the diversification of the AFV. This will give the reader a good insight into why the armoured fighting vehicle played an increasingly important role in the land battles of the first half of the 20th century.

ABOVE LEFT: **A pair of M8 75mm/2.95in Howitzer Motor Carriages, clearly showing the exposed position of the gun crew. The vehicle was based on a modified M5 chassis and was well liked by its crews.** TOP: **The Troop Carrier/Supply Mk IX Tank was a first attempt at an armoured personnel carrier. Entering service in October 1918, it was too late to have a significant impact on the progress of the war.** ABOVE: **An early four-wheel Lanchester Armoured Car of the RNAS. This vehicle was based on the Lanchester Sporting Forty touring car chassis.**

Key to flags

For the specification boxes, the national flag that was current at the time of the vehicle's use is shown.

🏴	Belgium	🏴	Italy
🏴	Canada	🏴	Japan
🏴	Czechoslovakia	🏴	South Africa
🏴	France	🏴	UK
🏴	Germany	🏴	USA
🏴	India	🏴	USSR

The History of Armoured Fighting Vehicles

In 100 years, the armoured fighting vehicle has undergone many transformations. The first vehicles were created by designers who were unsure of what it was that the army required, or indeed how to produce a machine that would usefully replace the horse. Once armies had acquired useful vehicles, they then spent the next 30 years learning how to use these new weapon systems. Men such as Sir Basil Henry Liddell Hart and Heinz Guderian would be fundamental in devising and developing the theory of mechanized warfare.

In 1914, armoured vehicles were improvised using boiler plate to protect the underlying commercial vehicle chassis. Once the usefulness of these conversions had been demonstrated, designs were quickly drawn up for purpose-built vehicles. By the end of World War I, the three main types of AFV had emerged. In the years that followed, the AFV became an established part of the Armoured Division, with many specialized vehicles developed in response to tactical and technological developments. By the end of World War II, the application of mass production methods resulted in vast numbers of vehicles being produced, as well as a profusion of types and their variants.

LEFT: **The American DUKW served in many different theatres in World War II. Here "Pistol Packen Mama" takes US troops over the Rhine in 1945.**

LEFT: **In 1902, F. R. Simms designed and built a "war car" which had a crew of five. One man drove the vehicle while two operated the Maxim 1pdr "pom-pom" gun in the rear and two men operated the two forward machine-guns.**
BELOW: **One of the early development vehicles designed to act as an infantry fighting vehicle. Made from an old steam boiler, the cab and engine were also covered in boiler plate. The engine was not powerful enough to handle the weight of all this armour.**

Evolution

Probably the earliest significant use of the AFV was in 1125 when the army of the Sung dynasty halted the advance of the invading Tartar forces in Northern China using iron-plated armoured "cars" to break up the Tartar cavalry. The next time that AFVs make an appearance on the battlefield is between 1420 and 1431 during the peasant rebellion in Bohemia (the modern Czech Republic). Jan Zizka led a peasant army of 25,000 against the might of the 200,000-strong Imperial German army. Zizka came up with the idea of putting sheets of iron on some of his wagons. Inside were men armed with handguns, crossbows and large axes and could fire from the wagons through slits in the iron plates.

The AFV did not come into its own until the 20th century, with each type developing separately. First was the armoured car, followed by the Self-Propelled Gun (SPG) and finally the infantry carrier. Mr F. R. Simms, a British motoring enthusiast, came up with the idea of mounting a machine-gun on the front of a quadricycle and installing a small petrol engine at the rear. The Simms machine was widely publicized and spurred others on to design "war cars" of one sort or another, and even Henry Ford got in on the act and mounted a machine-gun on the front of a Model T. France produced a Charron armoured car in 1906 and a Hotchkiss car in 1909. These were basic touring cars with a sheet of armour bent around the tonneau. These early machines represent the first attempts to bring a new measure of speed and mobility to the battlefield.

SPGs made slow progress. The first ones to be developed were mobile anti-balloon guns such as the German Rheinmetall of 1909. The idea of these vehicles was to provide a highly mobile defensive force, capable of rapid deployment against a very mobile enemy. By December 1914, trenches ran from the Swiss border to the North Sea and siege warfare had started. In Britain there were no mobile Anti-Aircraft (AA) guns at the start of World War I, so a crash programme was put in place. The 5.9kg/13lb gun, weighing 457kg/9cwt was placed on Thorneycroft and Peerless trucks as a makeshift response, but once established it built up a sound reputation. When the rains came to the Flanders area and the earth turned into a sea of mud, horse-drawn transport with its narrow steel-rimmed wheels ground to a halt. In particular, the movement of guns was almost impossible. After a successful attack, the infantry would be without close artillery support, as horse-drawn artillery could not cross the mud of No Man's Land. They needed this support to keep the momentum of the attack going. As a result, Gun Carrier Tanks were developed and an order for 48 units was placed. They arrived in France in 1917 but were only deployed a few times before being relegated to the supply role. The main problem was that these new vehicles did not fit the established way of handling guns in the British Army, namely, with horse teams.

For centuries, the infantry have had to march to the battlefield and then go into battle on foot. Railways were to change the face of warfare in Europe, by enabling armies to move over large distances very quickly and to arrive on the battlefield in good order. The Franco-Prussian War of 1870–71 was the first example of transportation by rail. In 1914, the French garrison of Paris was loaded into taxis and moved to the front to help stop the German advance. The British Army came up with the idea of moving troops to the front line by putting them into imported London buses, the sides of which were covered in heavy timber to give the troops some protection from shell splinters. In 1917, the British Army asked for a supply tank that could carry 10.16 tonnes/10 tons of supplies or 30 armed men. Being a converted tank, it could keep up with a tank assault and deliver the infantry into the German lines. The first of these machines did not arrive in France until October 1918, in readiness for the attacks planned for 1919, which were to prove to be unnecessary.

TOP: **F. R. Simms demonstrates his Quadricycle Maxim Gun Carrier at Roehampton in 1898. The ammunition was carried in a tray under the gun. The manoeuvrability of the machine left a lot to be desired.** ABOVE: **A British idea for a "war car" designed in 1855. Called the Cowen Battle-Car, it had several retractable scythes fitted to the sides of the vehicle.** BELOW: **The armoured traction engine of Fowler's Armoured Road Train. This was sent to South Africa in 1902 during the Boer War to pull armoured wagons full of British troops. The idea did not work as well as expected.**

ABOVE: **The Holzschuher car of 1558 was conceived as a mobile "war car" that would be pulled into position by a team of horses, unhitched and left to pour fire into the flanks of an enemy.**

"Operations of war require 1,000 fast chariots, 1,000 four-horse wagons covered in leather and 100,000 mailed troops. Now when an army marches abroad the treasury will be empty at home."
Sun Tzu, c.500–320 BC

World War I

The story of the AFV in World War I is the story of the armoured car, and in particular its use by the British Royal Naval Air Service (RNAS). When the Germans overran Belgium in 1914, they came up against a few improvised armoured cars being used by the Belgian Army. These vehicles, the first AFVs to see action, were basic touring cars with boiler plate fitted to them and armed with one or two machine-guns. They did excellent work in slowing the German advance. The RNAS based at Dunkirk had 18 cars for aircraft support and downed-pilot rescue, and, on hearing about the Belgian success with armouring touring cars, armed two of their own and used them effectively against German cavalry.

The RNAS continued producing these home-made armoured cars and the Royal Naval Armoured Car Division (RNACD) was officially formed in October 1914, taking part in the land battles in Flanders over the next year. The Division would eventually consist of 15 armoured car squadrons and a Divisional HQ. Each armoured car squadron consisted of three sections, each with four cars. The Navy pushed on converting more and more vehicles including several trucks, but this led to problems with maintenance and spare parts. A basic armoured body with full body and overhead protection and mounting a turret with 360-degree traverse was developed so that it could be fitted to several makes of car. The two main chassis used were the Rolls-Royce and the Lanchester. The first of these new designs started arriving in France by Christmas 1914.

> "'The Chase' was the unit's especial type of war, and went into it with all the dash and efficiency that its long training had produced."
> RNAS Armoured Car Section Commander, 1915

TOP: **One of the British Gun Carriers developed to move heavy guns forward after a successful attack in World War I. The two-wheel trailer at the rear of the vehicle was to aid steering, but this idea was quickly dropped. The doors in the rear of the vehicle are the main entrance and exit for the gun crew.**
ABOVE: **A British RNAS Seabrook armoured car of 1915. This 10,160kg/10-ton vehicle had a crew of six and was armed with a 3pdr gun and a Vickers machine-gun. All these early RNAS vehicles were built as "one-offs". Most were later handed over to the British Army.**

Once the Western Front had settled into stagnant trench warfare, there was very little for the RNACD to do and in October 1915 the last section returned to Britain for re-assignment. RNACD squadrons Nos.3 and 4 were first redeployed to Gallipoli, where they did nothing, and then to Egypt, where the British Army reluctantly took charge of them and used them for patrolling the Suez Canal and in western desert operations. The army broke up the naval units and formed the Light Armoured Motor (LAM) Batteries of the Motor Machine Gun Corps, standardizing on the Rolls-Royce armoured car as it was very reliable. The British Army in

FAR LEFT: **London buses shipped over to France were used to move British troops up to the front line. At first they carried their London bus livery, but this was quickly removed along with all the window glass.**
ABOVE: **The front view of the British Gun Carrier. The driver's station is on the left and the vehicle commander's on the right, with the field gun in the middle, mounted on its carriage from which the wheels have been removed.**
BELOW: **Senior British officers inspecting a line-up of Royal Naval mobile anti-aircraft guns. The guns mounted on these vehicles are French 75mm/2.95in AA guns.** BOTTOM: **British officers inspecting a Thorneycroft mobile anti-aircraft gun. These vehicles were formed into mobile brigades and were moved around the battlefield to cover any major attack.**

general was not sure how to deploy the armoured car but individual officers discovered their worth and used them with imagination and panache. The desert proved to be an excellent operational area for the armoured car, but it also had significant success against German forces in German South West Africa and British East Africa. No.1 squadron RNACD, which was sent to Russia in June 1916 to help fight the Germans in that country, had covered 85,295km/53,000 miles from the White Sea to the Crimea in their operations by the time of their return to Britain after the Russian surrender in late 1917.

The armoured car also showed its value in India, particularly on the Northern Frontier, where demand for troops in other theatres had weakened the forces used for peacekeeping. Armoured vehicles of all types were found to be a very satisfactory substitute for both infantry and cavalry against marauding tribesmen. Armoured cars had speed and endurance, and could be adapted to suit local conditions. One was even fitted with a ten-barrelled Gatling gun, while others had pom-pom guns fitted. Some trucks were converted to the SPG role having 76mm/2.99in guns fitted to them.

Other AFV developments of World War I were comparatively minor. They included early SPGs – guns mounted on trucks for mobile Anti-Aircraft (AA) defence, such as the Thorneycroft, or in the support role for armoured car operations. One tracked SPG was developed by the British but only used a few times, as it did not conform to standard army procedure. Infantry carriers were under development and if the war had gone on into 1919 would have been deployed in action against the Germans. All of these were minor developments compared to the armoured car, and it was undoubtedly due to the ingenuity of the RNAS that the armoured car played such an important role in World War I.

Between the wars

After the developments in armoured vehicles by France and Britain during World War I, many military men felt that the days of the horse were numbered, and between 1920 and 1939 there was a general move towards the mechanization of armed forces. Britain continued to build and experiment with more tanks, armoured cars and carriers than any other nation and would lead the world for many years in this development. French and British light tanks and armoured cars would be sold to many countries, becoming the nucleus of many virgin armoured units. In 1929 Britain made two significant developments in the use of the AFV: the fitting of short-range two-way radios to all AFVs, and the development and use of the smoke mortar, both of which would become standard equipment in practically all armies.

Under the Treaty of Versailles that ended World War I, Germany was not allowed to build any AFVs. They were allowed unarmed armoured cars for policing duties, and some of these were borrowed by the army for exercises. Nevertheless, some tanks and armoured cars were built secretly both in Germany and in a German-controlled factory in Sweden, and a German-Soviet pact enabled the Germans to open a testing establishment in Kazan in 1926. Heinz Guderian made the most of this test area and companies like Daimler-Benz, Rheinmetall and Bussing sent armoured cars and other AFVs for testing. By 1927–28 the Germans had developed a number of very good half-track vehicles for towing artillery. Although Guderian had most of the components of an armoured division either in place or under development by 1936, it would not be until the spring of 1939 that the armoured half-track Sd Kfz 251 infantry carrier would start to come into service.

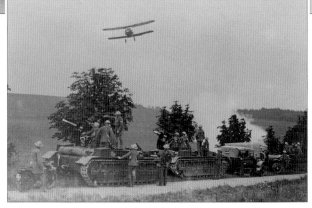

TOP: **In 1928, Vickers Armstrong were experimenting with the idea of the wheel-cum-tracked vehicle. The vehicle in the picture has the tracks deployed and is armed with a single Vickers machine-gun. Only two machines were built.** ABOVE: **Two Birch Gun SPAAGs of 20 Battery deployed on the roadside during an exercise on Salisbury Plain. These vehicles were not very reliable and were quickly dropped by the British Army.**

Russia had bought a large number of British armoured cars during World War I and more were sent to aid the White Russians, but these early cars had great problems with the rough Russian roads and were badly maintained by the Russian peasants who used them. The Soviet Union developed several very good armoured cars and other AFVs in this period, but not armoured infantry carriers and SPGs. The Soviets felt that the infantry could travel on the outside of the tanks, as with almost unlimited manpower life was cheap – Mother Russia was all.

The Americans sat back and did practically no AFV development between 1919 and 1930. There was great debate between the cavalry and the infantry over what they wanted and how it was going to be used. However, between 1930 and 1939, development went into overdrive and 48 projects were

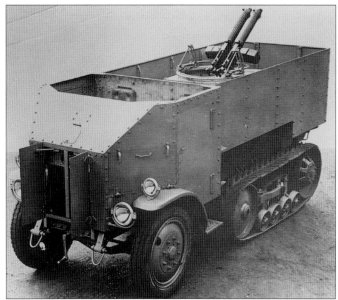

ABOVE: **A Light Tank Mk II fitted with collapsible pontoons. The exhaust pipe on the left has been raised and the driver's visor has been smeared with sealant. The man on the rear of the vehicle is operating the outboard motor, which was attached to the rear of the tank.**

on trials with the army, but only six would eventually see service. With the start of World War II, the Americans very quickly discovered that they had been left far behind by developments in Britain and Germany and so they swiftly set about improving the standard of the AFVs in service with the US Army.

Italy had undertaken some armoured car development during World War I, but this was now considerably increased by the Fiat Company. In addition, the Italians had bought several of the new Carden-Loyd small fast tanks from Britain.

By the end of World War I it was considered very desirable to have SPGs and they were under development in many countries but few would see service, like the Birch guns in the British Army. It would not be until 1940 that the first real SPG would appear. In the meantime the Portee was developed. This was a basic truck that the small field gun or anti-tank gun would be winched up on to. There was room for the gun crew on the vehicle, which would be driven to where the gun was required. The gun and crew would then leave the vehicle that would move off to a place of safety.

Many traditionally inclined army officers and men around the world had been greatly opposed to the introduction of mechanization and the loss of the horse, but nothing could withstand the power of the armoured formation which Guderian and his Panzer Divisions would demonstrate to the world with the invasion of Poland in 1939.

TOP: **An armoured Burford-Kegresse machine-gun carrier B11E5. It was based on the company's 1,524kg/30cwt half-track chassis. The gun-mounting could be removed and the vehicle turned into a personnel carrier.** ABOVE: **The Burford-Kegresse Half-track Portee vehicles of the 9th Light Battery. The 94mm/3.7in howitzers are carried complete on the rear of the vehicle. The loading ramps can also be seen on the rear deck.** BELOW: **An Indian Pattern armoured car and a Crossley Mk 1 on display at the Bovington Tank Museum. These large armoured cars were developed to help police the Empire, especially in areas such as the North West Frontier in India.**

> "The German system consists essentially of making a breach in the front with armour and aircraft, then to throw mechanized and motorized columns into the breach."
> General A. Armengaud (analysis of the Blitzkrieg on Poland), 1939

Dad's Army

After the withdrawal of British and French forces from Dunkirk in June 1940, there was a real threat that the Germans would invade Britain once France had been defeated. There was a great shortage of AFVs in Britain as the British Expeditionary Force (BEF) had left all its heavy equipment behind so an urgent programme of rearmament was started. In the meantime, a number of makeshift designs were used, based on standard civilian saloon cars and trucks.

Many Home Guard units produced their own armoured cars. Some were very good and would have performed well against the enemy, but most were death traps to their users and would have been all too easily brushed aside by the Germans. One unit based at Chiswick in London converted several buses, by removing the bus bodywork and replacing it with a steel shell that had several firing slits in it. These unorthodox armoured cars and trucks were officially discouraged by the high command as they did not fit into the designated role of the Home Guard and the use of these unsupported AFVs would have been a disaster. Two of the better armoured cars were the Beaverette and the Humberette, based on the standard Humber Super Snipe chassis, built at the insistence of Lord Beaverbrook (the Beaverette was named after him). Sir Malcolm Campbell, the land and water world speed record holder, was the provost company commander of the 56th London Division, Home Defence Force, and he designed and then built the prototype of the Dodge armoured car which was

unofficially known as the "Malcolm Campbell" car. Seventy of these were built by Briggs Motor Bodies of Dagenham and were ready by the end of August 1940. To increase the fire-power of these cars and trucks, the Home Guard would often fit captured German machine-guns from crashed bombers to their vehicles, the only problem being fresh supplies of ammunition! Some units managed to get hold of a few World War I 6pdr tank guns and fitted them to the Malcolm Campbell cars.

ABOVE: **Two 762kg/15cwt civilian vehicles converted for the use of the Home Defence Force in 1940. Each vehicle has a crew of three, one driver and two for the single machine-gun mounted in the open-topped rear.**
BELOW: **A Humber saloon car converted for the Home Guard. Six men could be carried in the vehicle. The windows have been removed and replaced with metal plates with a firing slit cut in them.**

"Armadillos" were a large group of AFVs designed and built by the London Midland and Scottish Railway (LMS) workshop at Wolverton. Several prototypes were developed using different types of boiler plate as armour, but these were rejected in favour of a wooden box structure. The wooden box armour was made up as a sandwich with 76mm/3in wooden planks front and back, with a 152mm/6in thick filling of gravel between the planks. The box had an open top with an AA machine-gun mount and all-round armoured firing slits in the sides, and was bolted to the flat bed of many different types of truck. It was proof against small arms fire but nothing else. The cab had the glass removed and mild steel plate inserted which gave the driver some protection but was not bullet-proof. Some 700 Armadillos of three different marks were built. Concrete was also used as armour on several types of truck, known as "Bison". These were bullet-proof and proof against small anti-tank rounds and were basically concrete pillboxes mounted on truck flat beds. The Beaver Eel, known to the RAF as "Tender, Armoured, Leyland Type C", was built by Leyland for the protection of aircraft factories and airfields. These vehicles were based on the Leyland Retriever 3-ton truck and by the end of September 1940, Leyland had produced 250 and LMS 86 of this type. The last major conversion type was the Bedford type OXA which was officially the "Lorry, 30cwt, Armoured Anti-Tank,

ABOVE LEFT: **A heavy truck chassis has been used for this large armoured infantry carrier. This conversion has been carried out by the LMS workshops. It carried a crew of two plus an infantry section of ten men.** ABOVE: **A civilian 1,524kg/30cwt truck converted into an armoured car in 1940. It has been named "Flossie" by the crew. The vehicle had a crew of eight and was armed with a single light machine-gun and small arms. Only the driver's position was equipped with a visor.**

Bedford". These had a custom-made armoured cab and body for the truck and were fitted with the Boys anti-tank rifle and several machine-guns. All these truck conversions could take up to five men in the fighting compartment and some of the larger conversions could take a full section of ten men.

By the summer of 1942 as the threat of invasion diminished and more conventional vehicles were available, all the truck conversions had reverted back to their normal role, and the light armoured cars were by now relegated to airfield defence, some even being passed over to the American 8th Air Force.

ABOVE: **A Humber Saloon car being used by the British Home Guard in 1940. This car has had a hatch cut in the roof above the passenger's seat and a larger removable hatch over the rear section so the men in the back could stand up and fire from the car.** RIGHT: **A Bedford 1,524kg/30cwt truck converted and issued to the British Army in 1940. This vehicle was called a Lorry Armoured Anti-Tank as the vehicle carried a Boys anti-tank rifle and light machine-guns.**

The coming of age of the Self-Propelled Gun

The SPG is a motorized or tracked artillery piece which unlike the tank does not have to be in visual range of its target. A number of countries had tried SPGs before World War II but nothing had come of it, either because they were not reliable or because they did not conform to basic army modes of operation. The rise of the SPG can be attributed to the impact of the tank on the battlefield, as demonstrated by Guderian's new formation that swarmed all over Poland, France, and later the Soviet Union. Supporting forces now had to move at the same speed as the tank and go where the tank went. Two distinct ideologies of how the SPG should be used in action came to the fore during World War II. One regarded the SPG as an extension of basic artillery doctrines, developing and using these guns as platforms to deliver indirect supporting fire in the usual way. The other school believed that the SPG should be used as a mobile gun to deliver close support to armour, and this theory, favoured by the Germans, led to the development of the Assault Gun.

Guderian knew he needed an SPG to support his tanks and infantry. The Germans started development in 1938 of the 15cm/5.91in sIG on a Panzer I chassis. This was an infantry

> **"Unleash the God of War!"**
> Marshal Zhukov's order to the Soviet artillery in front of Berlin, 1945

gun mounted on top of the tank chassis with very basic protection and first saw action during the invasion of France in 1940. The Germans would go on to produce some very good SPG mounts and some extraordinary mounts that were just plain crazy. The largest production run was for the Sturmgeschutz III, often mistaken for a tank, as it very often had to fill the role of the tank. As the war turned against Germany there was a mad scramble to get more and more guns on self-propelled mounts.

By 1941 there was an urgent need for SPGs for the British forces, both for the Home Defence Forces and for the 8th Army in the deserts of North Africa. For the Home Forces, the Churchill 76.2mm/3in Gun Mk 1 was developed. An order for 100 vehicles was placed but only 24 were produced before the order was cancelled. They were very quickly transferred to the training role and did not see action. The Bishop was developed for the British 8th Army, with which it would see extensive service in North Africa and later in Sicily. These guns were very quickly phased out of service by the American M7, which in turn was replaced by the Sexton.

Like the Germans, the Italians very quickly took to the idea of the SPG and put it into production and service with the Italian Army. The majority of the Italian SPGs were known as Semovente. These were very good vehicles and were also used in large numbers by the Germans. They were used to equip several reformed Italian units after World War II.

The Japanese were well behind in the development of armour compared to the other combatants of World War II and even further behind in the development of the SPG. They did come up with a few designs but these were never produced in any large numbers. The most numerous type was the Type 4 HO-RO 150mm/5.91in SPG. These vehicles were hand-built and no production facility was ever set up. Very few records survive about these vehicles in action and deployment.

After the destruction of the Soviet armoured forces during the German invasion of the Soviet Union in June 1941 (Operation "Barbarossa"), the Russians had to start rebuilding their armoured formations almost from scratch. They took the idea of the SPG to heart and produced it in great numbers, concentrating on the assault gun types as these fitted into Soviet armed forces doctrine better than the indirect artillery support of Western design.

World War II would see the meteoric rise of the SPG both as an important weapon system in its own right and as part of the armoured formation, and would go on to replace the towed gun in many armed forces around the world.

TOP LEFT: **A British prototype SPG developed during World War II that never went into production. The chassis was from a Crusader tank and the gun was a 140mm/5.51in medium gun.** TOP RIGHT: **An Italian mobile anti-aircraft vehicle developed in 1915. A Lancia I Z lorry chassis was used with a 75/30 gun mounted on the rear. There was only room for the driver and gun commander on the vehicle, the rest of the crew travelling in a separate one.** ABOVE LEFT: **A Carden-Loyd Mk VI carrier armed with a 47mm/1.85in gun. Development started in 1927. However, the British Army preferred the machine-gun armed carrier, so the 47mm/1.85in version was only sold abroad.** ABOVE RIGHT: **An American prototype SPAAG vehicle. The T53E1 used the Sherman tank chassis and mounted a 90mm/3.54in anti-aircraft gun. The top of the turret was open to allow for maximum elevation of the gun and the vehicle had four stabilizers fitted to the running gear.** BELOW: **The rear of the AMX GCT 155mm/6.1in SPG. The chassis of this vehicle is the AMX-30 MBT. The rear ammunition bins hold 42 mixed rounds, which can be reloaded in about 30 minutes. It has a crew of four.**

LEFT: **A DUKW, usually pronounced "Duck", emerging from the water on to an Italian beach. It has its trim vane raised on the front of the vehicle. Derived from the GMC 6x6 2,540kg/2.5-ton truck, but fitted with a boat-shaped hull, a total of 21,000 of these vehicles were built.**
BELOW: **A DUKW on shore in hostile territory. This vehicle has been fitted with a machine-gun mount above the co-driver's position. Operating the machine-gun was very dangerous as there was no protection for the gunner.**

Amphibious Infantry Assault Vehicles

There are several ways for a vehicle to cross a water obstacle such as a river; it can go over a bridge, be ferried across by boat, swim across under its own power or drive across the river bed fully submerged and out the other side. For amphibious landings on an enemy coastline, vehicles have to swim ashore under their own power or be landed by special landing craft.

Amphibious vehicles did not make an appearance until World War II, but since then great strides have taken place in many armoured forces around the world. During World War II there were many variations on a theme, some vehicles being designed to carry loads from ship to shore while others were designed to take a section of 35 men and put them on a beach. A British idea for producing an amphibious tank involved using a flotation screen, which was also used on several post war vehicles. At first the DD (Duplex Drive) Sherman tank (as these first models were known) were not liked by the Navy and it took the intervention of General Eisenhower himself to get the project moving. Eventually, some 300 of these tanks were built to take part in the D-Day invasion.

The Americans were to produce two of the best and most numerous amphibious vehicles of the war, both of which would soldier on for many years after it finished. The first was the DUKW amphibious truck based on the GMC 6x6 2,540kg/2.5-ton truck – one of the most important weapons of World War II as far as General (later President) Eisenhower was

concerned. The letters DUKW (pronounced "Duck") explain the vehicle's specification. D stands for a 1942 vehicle, U is for amphibious, K indicates that it is all-wheel drive and W denotes that it has twin rear axles. Most of these vehicles were not armoured, but some were converted into special support vehicles, like the rocket-firing version known as the Scorpion, while others had field guns firing from the cargo area. The second vehicle was the Landing Vehicle Tracked (LVT) which was to play a very important role in the island-hopping campaign in the Pacific and in the crossing of the last great water barrier in Europe: "The Rhine Crossing". The LVT was to be found in many different variations from the basic troop transport and cargo carrier to vehicles fitted with tank turrets

LEFT: **A DUKW entering the Rhine and about to take American troops over into Germany. The DUKW had a central tyre inflation system so the driver could raise or lower tyre pressures from the driving position.** ABOVE: **An LVT (A) 1 demonstrating its full firepower during a night exercise. The vehicle had a crew of six and was armed with one 37mm/ 1.46in gun, one 12.7mm/50cal machine-gun in a turret and two 7.62mm/30cal machine-guns in pits behind the turret.**

giving close support to the invading forces. These vehicles would remain in service with armed forces around the world until the 1970s.

The Germans and the Japanese both dabbled in developing amphibious vehicles, the Germans with greater success. They produced a very effective amphibious version of the Kubelwagen called the *Schwimwagen* which proved to be a very useful vehicle. They also tried to give tanks like the Panzer III *Tauchpanzer* a snorkel device and converted some 168 vehicles, which were used once in 1941 at the crossing of the river Bug in Soviet Russia. The Japanese went for amphibious tanks such as the Type 2 Ka-Mi light tank developed by the Japanese Navy. Used several times very successfully, the big problem, as with all Japanese armour, was the lack of numbers, and so these were used in penny packets. Most ended their life as dug-in pillboxes on various Pacific islands.

During the "Cold War", NATO forces went for specialized armoured vehicles to bridge water obstacles, while the Soviet forces concentrated on amphibious vehicles. The Soviets designed and produced vehicles such as the BMP-1, BTR-60, 2S1 and the SA8 – a whole family of amphibious vehicles that used a water jet propulsion system when in the water. The main battle tanks use the snorkel system and take a large amount of time to ready for the water crossing, but once ready are driven into the river and the crew and engine draw air into the vehicle down the snorkel tube. The largest amphibious force in the world is the US Marine Corps which performs spearhead-style operations for the American Army but also act as an independent force when required.

ABOVE: **The LVT was also used by the British Army where it was known as the Buffalo. These two Buffalos are being loaded with Universal Carriers.**
BELOW: **Seven British LVT Buffalos are being readied for an operation to cross the Rhine. These vehicles are armed with three machine-guns and a single 20mm/0.79in cannon, and had a crew of four.**

Wartime developments

Great strides in AFV design and development were taken during World War II. The SPG went from a makeshift development into a sophisticated weapon system in the Allied armies, while the Axis forces scrambled to place as many guns as possible on to tracked or wheeled chassis. The British Army ended World War II with the medium 25pdr Sexton and the M40 155mm/6.1in heavy gun as the main SPGs and these would remain in service until the early 1960s. The Americans had several new designs in development at the end of the war that came into service during the 1950s.

The infantry carrier started as a lightly armed and armoured vehicle and was only capable of taking troops to the edge of the fighting. The British and Canadians came up with the idea of using the redundant SPG Priest vehicles in this role – by removing the gun and plating over the opening 12 men could be carried in safety. These were known as "unfrocked Priests" and were first used by the Canadians during their attack on Caen in 1944. The British also used a redundant tank chassis as an armoured infantry carrier. The Kangaroo, as it was called,

TOP: **A Morris Commercial C9/B portee armed with a 40mm/1.58in Bofors AA gun. The seats and windscreen could be folded forward to give the gun a full 360-degree traverse. It had a crew of four.**

ABOVE: **A 6pdr (57mm) anti-tank gun portee. This vehicle was a conversion of a Bedford truck. It is passing a burnt-out Panzer IV in North Africa during a British advance in 1942.**

was a conversion of the Canadian Ram tank; by removing the turret and the internal fittings there was room for ten men. Two regiments were kitted out with this vehicle and some 300 of these were used in north-west Europe by the Allies. In Italy, the Allies converted a further 177 vehicles. The one big disadvantage was that the infantry had to disembark over the top of the vehicle leaving them very exposed to enemy fire; this and other faults would be rectified in post-war development. The Russians did not develop any form of Armoured Personnel Carrier (APC) during World War II, feeling that the infantry could ride on the outside of the tank, and it would not be until the 1950s that they would start to develop APCs. The Americans looked at the Kangaroo and could see its shortcomings so stayed with the half-track infantry carrier until the mid-1950s.

> "Behind this armoured and mechanized onslaught came a number of German divisions in lorries."
> Winston Churchill (description of Blitzkrieg in France), June 1940

The armoured car had started World War II for the Allies as a small vehicle that was fast but poorly armed and armoured. They learnt quickly, and bigger and better cars did come into service by the war's end. In Britain they came up with the idea of making a wheeled version of the Sherman tank called the Boarhound. This was an eight-wheeled monster, 6.1m/20ft long and weighing 26,416kg/26 tons, which never went into service. The Germans went down the road of developing their eight-wheeled armoured car even further and putting larger and larger guns on the same chassis. In America the M6 and M8 armoured cars had been developed and saw extensive service during the war and further development post-war until replaced by modern armoured cars in the 1960s.

The rocket was beginning to make a name on the battlefield with many armies during World War II, and a number of special vehicles were developed to carry this new weapon. The main players in the rocket weapon system were the Germans, Russians and the Americans. The Germans put several different types of rockets on various half-tracks, but the biggest was the Sturmmörser. The Russians developed the Katyusha rocket system and would go on to develop several other systems post-war. The Americans also developed several systems, one being the T34 Calliope mounted on the Sherman tank. They also developed the artillery rocket further and designed several new vehicles post-war.

One of the most important vehicles to be developed was the armoured command truck or tank. These were often only lightly armed with just machine-guns, but would carry several extra radio sets so that commanders could keep in touch with their fighting units in the front line. These vehicles were developed further post-war and now are even more important on the battlefield. The story of the AFV in World War II clearly demonstrates the principle that the pace of development of new weapons and vehicles is very fast during a time of war while in times of peace it is long and slow.

ABOVE: **A German Sd Kfz 263 heavy armoured radio car. Above it is the large frame aerial that on later vehicles was replaced by a rod aerial. It carried a long-range radio transmitter and receiver and had a crew of five. The turret was fixed and had a machine-gun fitted in the front.**

ABOVE MIDDLE: **Two British LVT Buffalos entering the Rhine. These vehicles were operated by the 79th Armoured Division. The rear machine-gun positions have gun shields to protect the gunners from enemy fire.** ABOVE: **Two DD (Duplex Drive) tanks being readied to take to the water as part of a training exercise. One of the flotation screens has been fully inflated while the other is about half-raised.** LEFT: **A German RSO fitted with a PaK40 75mm/2.95in anti-tank gun. Designed and built by Steyr, the gun was directly mounted without its wheels and trails on to the wooden body at the rear of the vehicle.**

> "Divisional reconnaissance units should be armoured and preferably contain 2-pounder guns."
> General Bartholomew, July 1940

The adaptation of soft-skin vehicles

The average soldier around the world is very good at adapting to local terrain and conditions, and at adapting his vehicles to do the same. This has gone on since motorized vehicles first appeared on the battlefield. The RNAS armoured car section was one of the first units to do this and were very good at this type of conversion. They did a number of local conversions of cars and trucks, and would scrounge, beg or borrow weapons which they would fit to whatever vehicle was suitable, for example, 6-pound naval guns fitted to Peerless trucks to give the armoured cars better support.

During World War II, there was wholesale conversion of vehicles, which started with the British forces after the withdrawal from France in 1940. The shortage of vehicles made the troops very ingenious at adapting what they could, and turning them into some form of AFV. The Home Defence forces and the Home Guard made many local conversions of vehicles, which were frowned upon and openly discouraged by high command but not stopped. The British 8th Army in North Africa became real experts in the local adaptation of soft-skin vehicles into AFVs. With the constant advance and retreat by opposing forces, large numbers of enemy vehicles fell into each other's hands. One unit in particular would make its name from its vehicle conversions: the Long Range Desert Group (LRDG). This group took vehicles such as the Chevrolet truck and the Jeep and fitted them with a large number of cannon and machine-guns. The Jeeps carried up to five heavy machine-

guns, while the trucks had the heavier weapons such as 20mm/0.79in cannon and several heavy machine-guns fitted. They then took these vehicles far behind the German lines and created havoc in the German supply routes. The LRDG worked very closely with another new unit called the Special Air Service (SAS), who would take their converted Jeeps into Sicily, Italy and finally into north-west Europe where they continued to work deep behind the German front line.

The Germans were better known for their conversion of captured enemy armour, but they did do a number of conversions to their half-tracks and other soft-skin vehicles, mounting various different types of captured field guns on them. A large number of these vehicles were used by the German *Afrika Korps* in the fast flowing mobile warfare conducted in the deserts of North Africa.

The Americans were and still are great innovators and converters of soft-skin vehicles. During World War II, they converted the Jeep from a light utility vehicle into a heavily armed AFV by fitting armour plate and numerous heavy machine-guns to the vehicle. Some were fitted with rocket launchers. During the Battle of the Bulge, the American paratroopers surrounded at Bastogne turned a number of Jeeps into armoured cars and used them as a mobile fire-fighting unit rushed to any position under great pressure from

ABOVE: **A British AEC 10,160kg/ 10-ton truck that has been converted into an SPG in 1940. A number of these vehicles were built to help bolster the coastal defences of Britain. They were armed with a range of obsolete naval guns.**
RIGHT: **An American pick-up truck has been converted into an AFV by fitting a single Lewis gun in the rear cargo area. The standard road wheels have been replaced with railway wheels so the vehicle can be used to patrol the railway.**

RIGHT: **HMS Aniche is a Talbot armoured car. This is a modified version of the first Admiralty Pattern vehicle that was built for the RNAS in 1914–15. There are two spare tyres on the rear of the vehicle.**
BELOW: **This bulldozer has been converted into an armoured vehicle by being covered with steel plate and having two machine-guns fitted to the front of the vehicle.**

a German attack. To put more rocket batteries into action the Americans mounted launch tubes on the back of "deuce and half" (GMC 2,540kg/2.5-ton) trucks. These trucks were also fitted with the M45 quad 12.7mm/50-caliber mounts to give supply convoys some protection from both air or ground attacks. In the island-hopping campaign of the Pacific war, the Jeep proved to be an excellent support AFV. Fitted with heavy machine-guns and rockets, it could go where other vehicles could not. During the Vietnam War, the Americans had a real shortage of armoured cars and other escort vehicles for their supply convoys which were constantly attacked. The men of the transport battalions started putting armour plate on some of their trucks, the favourite being the 5,080kg/5-ton M54A2. They then fitted them with a wide variety of weapons such as the M45 quad mount, mini guns. In a few cases, the complete hull of M113 APCs minus the tracks and running gear were placed on the back of the truck.

No matter where they are, troops will continue to adapt and convert their vehicles officially or unofficially to meet local circumstances, often with remarkable success.

ABOVE: **A line-up of three Austin vehicles. Two have been converted into AFVs by attaching steel plate around them. Each armoured car has an open roof so that a light machine-gun can be fitted on a pedestal mount. The middle vehicle is an ambulance.** BELOW: **An armoured 3,048kg/3-ton truck that has been converted into an APC using steel plate. The side-skirts covering the wheels are hinged to allow access to the tyres and fuel tank.**

A–Z of World War Armoured Fighting Vehicles

With the invention of the compression engine in 1892, military weapons developers around the world tried to fit it to various horseless carriages, resulting in some wonderful but impractical machines that were unusable on a battlefield.

The earliest practicable designs were produced in 1914 when the Belgian Army fitted machine-guns to touring cars which had been covered in boiler plate. These performed very well and were copied and developed further by the RNAS who used them aggressively in several different theatres. In World War II, the armoured car became the eyes of the armoured division.

There were a number of unsuccessful attempts to produce SPGs in World War I but it was not until World War II that this vehicle was really developed. Initially these were very crude conversions but by 1945, they had been developed into purpose-built, sophisticated weapons systems and had proved their worth on the battlefield.

The infantry carrier was developed in the 1930s from the early German half-track, which gave the infantry only basic protection, to the Kangaroo in the 1940s, which would give troops the protection of tank armour and allow them to fight alongside the tanks.

LEFT: **A column of British Bren gun carriers passing over a bridge.**

LEFT: **An LVT (A) 1 climbing out of the water. The rear machine-gun position can be seen manned behind the turret. This was a weakness as it let water into the vehicle.** ABOVE: **75mm LVT (A) 4 from above showing the position of the turret. The deck of the vehicle is fully covered, while the top of the turret is open to the elements. The ring mount for the 12.7mm/50cal machine-gun can be seen at the rear of the turret.**

75mm LVT (A) 4 Close Support Vehicle

The LVT (Landing Vehicle Tracked) was used for the first time in August 1942 during the amphibious operation to capture Guadalcanal. After this operation it was felt that some form of close support for the assault troops was required, and so in the Bougainville and Tarawa operations the LVTs were equipped with a number of machine-guns, typically three or four per vehicle. Following the Tarawa landings it was decided that a heavier support weapon was required and so the LVT Assault vehicle was developed and placed into production at the end of 1943. The LVT 2 chassis was used as the basis for a new vehicle called LVT (A) 1, which was completed by constructing the hull out of armour instead of mild steel, plating over the hull compartment and mounting a 37mm/1.46in M3 light tank turret, with two machine-gun positions in the rear of the vehicle behind the turret.

The LVT (A) 1 first saw action during the ROI-Namur invasion in January 1943 when 75 of these vehicles were used. They proved to be very effective but an even heavier weapon was required to give the Marines better close support, so development started on the LVT (A) 4. Production commenced in March 1943 with its first combat mission being the invasion of Saipan in June 1944. The new vehicle had the complete turret from the M8 GMC; this was fitted with a 75mm/2.95in short-range howitzer and a single 12.7mm/50cal machine-gun. The LVT (A) 4 could carry 100 rounds of 75mm/2.95in ammunition and 400 rounds for the machine-gun. The Continental engine was mounted in the rear of the vehicle and used 4.55 litres/ 1 gallon of fuel per 1.6km/1 mile.

Total production for the LVT (A) 1 was 509 vehicles, and when production of the LVT (A) 4 ended in 1945, 1,890 of these vehicles had been built. A number of rocket launchers and flamethrowers were fitted to both the LVT (A) 1 and the LVT (A) 4. The LVT (A) 4 would take part in the Korean War and remained in service with the US Marine Corps until the late 1950s, when it was replaced by the LVTH-6 105mm Tracked Howitzer.

LEFT: **A 75mm/2.95in LVT (A) 4 on a beach with the crew on or beside the vehicle. The protruding track grousers can be clearly seen; these propel the vehicle through the water and help it to move across soft sand.**

LVT (A) 4 Close Support Vehicle

Country: USA
Entered service: 1943
Crew: 6
Weight: 18,140kg/17.9 tons
Dimensions: Length – 7.95m/26ft 1in
    Height – 3.1m/10ft 2in
    Width – 3.25m/10ft 8in
Armament: Main – 75mm/2.95in M2/M3 howitzer
    Secondary – 1 x 12.7mm/0.5in machine-gun
    and 1 x 7.62mm/0.3in machine-gun
Armour: Maximum – 44mm/1.73in
Powerplant: Continental W-670-9A 7-cylinder
    186kW/250hp air-cooled radial petrol engine
Performance: Speed – Land 32kph/20mph;
    Sea 12kph/7mph
    Range – 240km/150 miles

LEFT: **One of the first AEC Mk 2 cars in North Africa in 1941. The sheer bulk of the vehicle can be clearly seen, but the vehicle appears to have none of the extra crew-storage fitted in the field by combat crews.** ABOVE: **An AEC Mk 3 moving through shallow water during landing trials. The vehicle commander is standing in the turret giving directions to the driver, who has limited vision from his position.**

AEC Armoured Car

This was designed as a private venture by the Associated Equipment Company Ltd, which normally made London buses. Information sent back from North Africa indicated a need for a heavyweight armoured car. AEC were also producing the very successful Matador gun tractor and so from July 1941 they produced the AEC Mk 1 using many of the Matador chassis parts. The armoured hull was a simple design and had a 2pdr gun and coaxial Besa machine-gun in a turret, the same turret as that used for the Valentine tank. One hundred and twenty Mk 1s were produced before the improved Mk 2 came along. This had a 6pdr gun in the turret, a more powerful engine, and the crew was increased from three to four. This was a big improvement but the army still wanted a bigger punch and so the Mk 3 was developed.

The Mk 3 had an improved hull and the British copy of the American M3 tank gun fitted in a new turret that had improved ventilation. However, when the driver was hull-down his only view of the outside was through a periscope which gave him very poor visibility. The driver could select either two-wheel drive

RIGHT: **The improved frontal design to aid in obstacle clearing can be seen. The driver's hatch is large and opens towards the turret, so the gun barrel has to be offset to the left to allow him to enter or leave the vehicle. Mounted between the wheels are large storage panniers.**

to the front axial only, which was used for long road journeys to save fuel, or four-wheel drive for cross country or combat. In total, 629 of these heavy armoured cars were built.

Most of the Mk 1 and Mk 2 cars were sent to the 8th Army and saw action in North Africa, Sicily and Italy. The Mk 3 was at first issued to armoured car units that were destined to be used in north-west Europe as heavy support vehicles to the other armoured cars, as it had double the thickness in armour in comparison to these. A number of the Mk 3 armoured cars were used by the Belgian Army after the war and remained in service well into the 1950s.

AEC Mk 3 Armoured Car	
Country: UK	
Entered service: 1942	
Crew: 4	
Weight: 12,903.2kg/12.7 tons	
Dimensions: Length – 5.61m/18ft 5in	
Height – 2.69m/8ft 10in	
Width – 2.69m/8ft 10in	
Armament: Main – M3 75mm/2.95in tank gun	
Secondary – Coaxial 7.7mm/0.303in Besa machine-gun	
Armour: Maximum – 30mm/1.18in	
Powerplant: AEC 6-cylinder diesel engine developing 116kW/155bhp	
Performance: Speed – 66kph/41mph	
Range – 402km/250 miles	

Archer 17pdr Self-Propelled Gun

In May 1942 the 17pdr anti-tank gun was approved for service. In June it was decided to mount this new gun on a self-propelled chassis to produce a tank destroyer. The first vehicle considered was the Bishop 25pdr SPG but this proved impracticable. The next was the Crusader tank but this was discarded due to reliability problems. Finally, it was decided to convert the Valentine chassis as used for the Bishop but with a different superstructure. However, there were a number of problems due to the length of the gun. This was mounted facing the rear and over the top of the engine deck of the vehicle in an open-topped fighting compartment, and had a limited traverse. A light steel roof was added to some vehicles at a later date, mainly post-war. Despite the length of the gun, a very compact vehicle with a low silhouette was produced. The fighting compartment was small for the four-man crew and 39 rounds of ammunition. The driver's position was left in the same place as it had been in the Valentine tank, but he could not remain in position when the gun was firing. The upper hull was of all-welded construction, with the lower hull, engine, transmission, and running gear being the same as on later Valentines. Secondary armament was the Bren gun, but no permanent mounting was provided on the vehicle. A popular crew conversion was to fit a 7.62mm/30cal Browning machine-gun to the front of the vehicle.

Firing trials were carried out in April 1943 and proved successful apart from a few minor changes. The vehicle was placed into priority production with an order for 800, but only 665 were produced, the first vehicle being completed in March 1944. It was issued at first to the anti-tank units of armoured divisions fighting in north-west Europe from October 1944. Later some were sent out to the 8th Army in Italy. While at first it was called the S-P 17pdr Valentine Mk 1, this was quickly dropped in favour of Archer.

TOP: **An Archer fitted with deep-wading gear. The large ducting on the rear deck allows the vehicle to draw air into the engine from above the level of the water.**
ABOVE: **The front is to the right, the small fighting compartment is in the middle and the engine in the rear of the vehicle with the gun barrel passing over it.**

LEFT: **Some of the ammunition storage can be seen on the right beside the 17pdr gun breach inside the small and cramped fighting compartment. Between the front of the vehicle and the gun breach is the driver's position.**

Archer 17pdr SPG

Country: UK
Entered service: 1944
Crew: 4
Weight: 18,796kg/18.5 tons
Dimensions: Length – 6.68m/21ft 11in
  Height – 2.24m/7ft 4in
  Width – 2.64m/8ft 8in
Armament: Main – 17pdr OQF (ordnance quick-firing) (76.2mm/0.3in) gun
  Secondary – 7.7mm/0.303in Bren machine-gun
Armour: Maximum – 60mm/2.36in
Powerplant: GMC M10 diesel 123kW/165hp
Performance: Speed – 24kph/15mph
  Range – 145km/90 miles

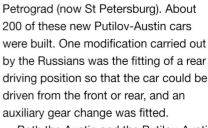

LEFT: **A pair of Austin cars travelling at speed. The large bulk of these vehicles and the twin offset turrets can be clearly seen. The Russians have placed armour plate next to the guns to protect the barrels.**
ABOVE: **An Austin armoured car in Russian service. The turret gunners are taking the opportunity to get some air as it is very cramped and stuffy inside the car. The driver has also dropped his visor for better vision and ventilation.**

Austin Armoured Car

Before the World War I, the Austin Motor Company Ltd was the largest supplier of cars and trucks to the Russian Imperial Army, and in 1913 won a contract to develop an armoured car for internal security duties in the large towns and cities. In 1914 an order was placed for 48 of these new armoured cars. The first armoured cars were built using the 22.4kW/30hp "Colonial" chassis, and had two machine-gun turrets mounted, one on each side of the rear of the vehicle. The wheels were all fitted with solid studded tyres. There were several problems with these early cars. Due to the height of the driver's cab, the machine-guns could not fire to the front and were too close side by side for the gun crews to operate them efficiently. The Russians also wanted to increase the thickness of armour on the vehicle. Consequently, a number of improvements were put into place by the Russians and Austin. A 37.3kW/50hp engine was fitted to the vehicle to cope with the increased weight and the tyres were made pneumatic with the rear axle having dual wheels. The turrets were offset to improve the fighting efficiency and the driver's cab was lowered so the guns could fire to the front.

Austin also sent the Russians a large number of chassis which had their bodies fitted in the Putilov works in Petrograd (now St Petersburg). About 200 of these new Putilov-Austin cars were built. One modification carried out by the Russians was the fitting of a rear driving position so that the car could be driven from the front or rear, and an auxiliary gear change was fitted.

Both the Austin and the Putilov-Austin were reliable cars, but like a number of early AFVs they suffered on the primitive Russian roads. In early 1917, all Austin production was switched to the Western Front and the 17th Battalion Tank Corps was equipped with these cars. The 17th Battalion with their Austins would lead the victorious British troops into Germany in November 1918.

LEFT: **In 1919, Britain urgently required armoured cars for duties in India and Ireland, so Austin-designed bodies were placed on other chassis. Peerless used their truck chassis to produce the Peerless 1919 Pattern armoured car.**

Austin/Putilov-Austin Armoured Car

Country: UK
Entered service: 1914
Crew: 5
Weight: 5,384kg/5.3 tons
Dimensions: Length – 4.88m/16ft
    Height – 2.4m/7ft 10in
    Width – 1.95m/6ft 5in
Armament: Main – 2 x 7.7mm/0.303in
    machine-guns
    Secondary – None
Armour: Maximum – 8mm/0.315in
Powerplant: 37.3kW/50hp Austin petrol engine
Performance: Speed – 50kph/31mph
    Range – 200km/125 miles

LEFT: **The rear driver's position visor is in the open position. Next to this is the rear-facing machine-gun. The hatch in the rear of the turret lifts up.**
ABOVE: **The AB 41 was an all-riveted construction. This could become lethal for the crew inside when the car was hit, as the rivets would burst loose and fly around the interior, wounding them.**

Autoblinda AB 41 Armoured Car

In 1939, the Italian Colonial Police and the Italian cavalry had a requirement for a new armoured car, so both needs were combined and in 1940 production began with the Autoblinda 40. This had a four-man crew and was armed with twin machine-guns in a turret and one facing the rear of the vehicle. There was also a plan to build small numbers of a version armed with a 20mm/0.79in cannon as a support vehicle. It was quickly discovered that the cannon armament was far better in service than the machine-gun only armament, so production of the AB 40 was stopped and the AB 41 took over.

The AB 41 used a turret very similar to that of the L6/40 light tank, and had a very advanced design for its time but suffered from one recurring problem with the four-wheel steering. The main armament was a Breda 20mm/0.79in modello anti-aircraft cannon with a coaxial machine-gun specially designed for use in AFVs. These vehicles could be fitted with a number of different wheels and tyres. One type was an extra wide sand tyre that was used when operating in areas such as North Africa. Another special feature was that the car could be fitted with wheels that would allow it to run on railway tracks. These were carried in the spare wheel area on the car and could be changed by the crew in less than 30 minutes. The vehicle had six forward and four reverse gears and two driving positions, so two of the crew were designated drivers. The AB 41 was produced in larger numbers than any other Italian armoured car during World War II.

By the time of the Italian surrender to the Allies in September 1943, nearly 400 of these vehicles had been produced. When the Germans took over the campaign against the Allies in Italy, they captured 57 of these vehicles and also retained the car's production, managing to produce a further 120 AB 41 armoured cars for their own use.

RIGHT: **The side entrance door to the crew compartment can be seen clearly in the rear of the raised body of the car. The armoured headlight covers are in the raised position exposing the large lights. The driver's vision slot is in between the lights and has a very limited field of vision.**

Autoblinda AB 41 Armoured Car

Country: Italy
Entered service: 1940
Crew: 4
Weight: 7,518kg/7.4 tons
Dimensions: Length – 5.20m/17ft 2in
    Height – 2.48m/8ft
    Width – 1.92m/6ft 4in
Armament: Main – 20mm/0.79in Breda modello 35 cannon
    Secondary – Coaxial 8mm/0.315in and rear 8mm/0.315in modello 38 air-cooled machine-guns
Armour: Maximum – 17mm/0.67in
Powerplant: 60kW/80bhp SAP Abn 6-cylinder water-cooled petrol engine
Performance: Speed – 78kph/49mph
    Range – 400km/248 miles

Autoblindo Mitragliatrice Lancia Ansaldo IZ

The first Lancia Ansaldo IZ armoured car was not armed and was used as an artillery spotting vehicle but in 1915 the vehicle was dramatically redesigned and turned into an armoured car. The first version was armed with a single machine-gun mounted in a circular turret, but this was soon upgraded to a twin mounting for machine-guns. Another type of turret was tried on the vehicle and this had a second smaller turret mounted on top of the larger bottom turret and each had a single machine-gun mounted, each with a 360-degree traverse. Another unique feature of these cars was the twin steel rails that made up the wire cutter that extended from the top of the driver's cab forward and down and ended in front of the radiator. The wheels on later versions of the vehicle were protected by armoured shields. The rear wheels were dual and the tyres were all pneumatic. Armoured firing ports were placed around the top of the crew compartment to allow the extra men in the crew to fire small arms from the vehicle. There was also a mounting for a rear-firing machine-gun in the crew compartment. It had good ground clearance, and there was a rack for a bicycle on the rear of the vehicle.

For most of World War I, the Italian armoured car units played very little part in the fighting against the Austro-Hungarian forces in the mountains in northern Italy. However, a number of

these cars were used to help stop the Austro-Hungarian and German forces breaking through in that area in 1917. Those captured by the Germans were used to equip armoured car units of their own. This vehicle was also used for training and equipping American troops in Italy. A large number of these cars were sent to North Africa on policing duties. They proved to be very durable and were used by the Italian Army in the Spanish Civil War between 1936–39. Total production was only 120 vehicles.

TOP: **Lancia armoured car fitted with the single large turret armed with twin machine-guns. The wire-cutter frame can be clearly seen fitted to the front of the vehicle. This structure was far from robust and easily damaged.** ABOVE: **A Lancia car fitted with two turrets, each armed with a single machine-gun. Both turrets can be operated independently and both can traverse through 360 degrees.**

LEFT: **A Lancia car in North Africa armed with three machine-guns, two in the large turret and one in the top turret. A large single headlight is mounted forward in the front of the vehicle. A number of these cars were still in service at the start of World War II.**

Autoblindo Mitragliatrice Lancia Ansaldo IZ

Country: Italy
Entered service: 1915
Crew: 6
Weight: 3,860kg/3.8 tons
Dimensions: Length – 5.40m/17ft 9in
　　Height – 2.40m/7ft 11in
　　Width – 1.82m/6ft
Armament: Main – 3 x Fiat machine-guns
　　Secondary – Small arms
Armour: Maximum – 9mm/0.354in
Powerplant: 26/30kW/35/40hp petrol engine
Performance: Speed – 60kph/37mph
　　Range – 300km/186 miles

BA-10 Armoured Car

By 1938, the Russians suspected that war with Germany was inevitable, despite political assurances to the contrary and the signing of the non-aggression pact between the Soviet Union and Germany. Consequently, a modernization of Soviet armoured vehicles was put in place. The BA-10 was already on the drawing board and would benefit from this acceleration in development. The vehicle used the GAZ AAA chassis, which was shortened and strengthened with the body being an all-welded construction. The main construction was done at the Izhorskiy plant where the body was built and then married to the GAZ chassis.

The BA-10 entered production in 1938 and would become the definitive as well as the most numerous form of the BA heavy armoured car. The layout was conventional with the engine at the front, driver and front gunner in the middle and a two-man turret at the rear. A modernized version of the BA-10 came into service in 1939, this improved design being called the BA-10M. The main improvements were an increase in armour for the vulnerable areas and a new 45mm/1.77in gun fitted in the turret – a simpler model with improved sights. The BA-10 and the BA-10M are often confused as there is very little difference between the two vehicles. The BA-10M has external fuel tanks mounted over the rear wheels and on both sides of the vehicle; these have often been mistaken for storage boxes. The BA-10 used the same turret as the BA-6 armoured car and was armed with the 45mm/1.77in M-1934 tank gun, together with a 7.62mm/0.3in DT machine-gun mounted

ABOVE: **Note the shelf on the rear of the BA-10 for the carriage of the "overall" tracks, which are used to improve its cross-country performance. The locking wires are still in place across the back of the vehicle.**

coaxially and another in the front of the car. The driver and front gunner sit side by side, with the vehicle commander and gunner in the two-man turret.

The BA-10/10M saw extensive service during the "Great Patriotic War" and large numbers of captured vehicles were put into service by the Finnish and German armies. Some 1,400 vehicles were produced of which 331 were the BA-10M version.

ABOVE: **A column of BA-10 cars. The crews are "buttoned up", but are not in a combat area as the radiator shutters are in the open position.**

ABOVE: **BA-10 cars in Poland in 1939, as Soviet crews show off their vehicles to German troops. Each car is carrying spare track-links on the side of the vehicle.**

BA-10 Armoured Car

Country: USSR
Entered service: 1938
Crew: 4
Weight: 5,080kg/5 tons
Dimensions: Length – 4.70m/15ft 5in
Height – 2.42m/7ft 11in
Width – 2.09m/6ft 7in
Armament: Main – 1 x 45mm/1.77in M-1934 tank gun and 1 x coaxial 7.62mm/0.3in DT machine-gun
Secondary – 7.62mm/0.3in DT machine-gun
Armour: Maximum – 15mm/0.59in
Powerplant: GAZ M1 4-cylinder 38kW/52hp petrol engine
Performance: Speed – 55kph/34mph
Range – 300km/186 miles

BA-20 Armoured Car

The BA-20 became the most numerous and popular armoured car in service with the Soviet Army in the late 1930s. Development for this car started at the GAZ factory in 1934 and under went trials in 1935. Once the vehicle had passed these trials it was accepted into service and placed into full production in late 1935.

The BA-20 used the GAZ M1 chassis which was built at the Novgorod factory, while the body was built at Vyksinskiy where the final assembly was also carried out. The original chassis had to be redesigned to accommodate the extra weight of the BA-20 body. The changes included a new differential and rear axle together with improvements to the suspension. The BA-20 normally carried

LEFT: **Captured BA-20 ZhD Drezine rail scout car. The Germans captured a number of these vehicles and used them to patrol the rear areas. A rail tow-link could be fitted to the spare wheel spigot to allow the car to be towed by a train.**

a crew of two but in the command version it had a crew of three. This was also the first Soviet armoured car to be fitted with an escape hatch in the floor of the vehicle. The BA-20 had an excellent cross-country performance and was especially good in soft going across marshy ground. The vehicle was also fitted with bullet-proof tyres and bullet-proof glass in the driver's vision block.

In 1938 the BA-20 was improved and became the BA-20M. It had a better turret and thicker armour and a three-man crew became standard. One interesting version of the BA-20 and the BA-20M was the ZhD. This car could change its road wheels for flanged steel railway wheels, which extended its range.

The BA-20 entered service in 1936 and remained in use until 1942, the BA-20M joining it from 1938 until 1942. The BA-20 first saw action in 1939 in the Battle of Khalkhin Gol against Japan, and later in the invasion of Poland and the Russo-Finnish war. The Finnish Army

TOP: **BA-20M armoured cars lined up in Moscow for the November Parade in 1940. The front row of cars are the command version as they have the radio aerial around the body of the vehicle.**
ABOVE: **The rear of the vehicle showing the single spare-wheel storage. This position was also used to store the rail-wheels.**

captured a number of these vehicles and put them back into service against the Russians. The Germans also captured a number of the BA-20M ZhD cars and used them for patrolling the rail network in an anti-partisan role. Both marks of the BA-20 proved to be very reliable and were well-liked by their crews.

BA-20 Armoured Car

Country: USSR
Entered service: 1936
Crew: 2 or 3
Weight: 2,341kg/2.3 tons
Dimensions: Length – 4.1m/13ft 5in
　Height – 2.3m/7ft 6in
　Width – 1.8m/5ft 9in
Armament: Main – 7.62mm/0.3in machine-gun
　Secondary – Small arms
Armour: Maximum – 6mm/0.24in
Powerplant: GAZ M1 4-cylinder 37kW/50hp
　petrol engine
Performance: Speed – 90kph/56mph
　Range – 350km/220 miles

LEFT: **The rear of a BA-64B. Above the spare wheel is the rear pistol port. The origins of the vehicle can be clearly seen, as the vehicle is an armoured Jeep. One defect of the BA-64B was a lack of adequate armament, so in 1943 the improved BA-64D was produced with the 12.7mm/0.5in heavy machine-gun.**

BA-64B Armoured Car

The first new Soviet armoured car design of World War II was the BA-64, designed and developed at the GAZ works. Production was started at the end of 1941 and went on until early 1942. This vehicle was based on the GAZ 64 Jeep. The vehicle had a coffin shape and an open pulpit-style machine-gun position, but production was slow due to the demands for the GAZ Jeep. A troop carrier version was developed but never put into production as it was too small and could only carry six men.

In 1943 GAZ started to produce a new Jeep and the BA-64B armoured car was developed by using this new chassis. It was a better vehicle than its predecessor

as it was more reliable and had a wider chassis, giving it a better cross-country ability. It had an all-welded construction with steeply angled plates to give some form of deflection to incoming munitions. This design idea was copied from German vehicles such as the Sd Kfz 221 and Sd Kfz 222. The BA-64B also had a small one-man turret fitted to the top of the vehicle. These changes constituted a big improvement on the BA-64, but the greatest single improvement was four-wheel drive. Total production of both vehicles was 9,110 and while production would finish in 1945, it would remain in service with the Soviet Army until 1956 and later still with Soviet allies.

Various versions of the basic vehicle were built, one of these being a command car that was fitted with a radio and map boards fixed on special frames built on the top of the vehicle with the turret removed. This vehicle became very popular with all ranks of officer as a basic battlefield run-about and taxi. In another unusual version, the wheels were removed; the front wheels were replaced with two heavy-duty skis and the rear wheels were replaced by a Kegresse half-track. A large number of the basic armoured cars were upgunned in the field by their crews with the installation of the DShK 12.7mm/0.5in heavy machine-gun and captured German machine-guns and cannon. Its crews nicknamed the vehicle the "Bobik". Many of these cars saw action in the Korean War.

LEFT AND ABOVE: **Late production BA-64Bs: the vehicle above has all its pistol ports open, and the driver's periscope can be seen attached to the front hatch.**

BA-64B Armoured Car

Country: USSR
Entered service: 1943
Crew: 2
Weight: 2,359kg/2.3 tons
Dimensions: Length – 3.67m/12ft 4in
　　　　　Height – 1.88m/6ft 2in
　　　　　Width – 1.52m/4ft 10in
Armament: Main – 7.62mm/0.3in machine-gun
　　　　　Secondary – Small arms
Armour: Maximum – 15mm/0.59in
Powerplant: GAZ MM 4-cylinder 40kW/54hp
　　　　　petrol engine
Performance: Speed – 80kph/50mph
　　　　　Range – 560km/350 miles

Beaverette Light Reconnaissance Car

After the withdrawal of the British Expeditionary Force from France in 1940, there was a proliferation of AFVs but only two were officially placed into production, one of these being the Beaverette. The vehicle was named after Lord Beaverbrook, Minister of Aircraft Production, on whose instance it was designed and placed into production within a few months.

The Beaverette was built by the Standard Motor Company Ltd of Coventry and used the chassis of the Standard 14 saloon car. The vehicle was covered in 11mm/0.43in mild steel, and was open topped, backed by 76.2mm/3in oak planks but with no rear protection for the crew. The driver had a small vision slot to the front and side, which was covered by sliding steel shutters and gave a very restricted field of vision. The Mk I had only just entered production when the improved Mk II was introduced. As the restrictions on steel were being lifted extra armour could be fitted to the Beaverette giving the crew some rear protection, and the radiator grille changed from vertical, as in the Mk I, to horizontal.

In 1941, the Mk III came into service. This was a very different vehicle and gave the crew all-round protection. Armour plate was now being made available and although the thickness was reduced to 10mm/0.394in, the whole vehicle was now covered in it, which gave it a rear-end-down attitude while being driven. The only entrance to the vehicle was through the single large door at the rear. In front of the driver was a step in the armour which placed the driver a little further back in the vehicle than the turret. In the final version, the Mk IV, the step was done away with and the driver now sat in front of the turret so that the machine-gun crew had more room to operate. These cars remained in service for many years and some which had been used for airfield defence were handed over to the Americans in 1942.

ABOVE LEFT: **A Beaverette Mk III armed with twin Vickers K machine-guns. The gunner is very exposed in this early turret. As well as the large opening in the front of the turret, the top is also open.**
ABOVE: **A column of Beaverette Mk I and II cars moving in convoy. The open-topped fighting compartment can be clearly seen. Because of this, the crew have to wear their steel helmets.**

LEFT: **The Beaverette Mk III with the single light machine-gun turret. This gave the gunner far better protection, but very poor vision. The large door in the rear of the Beaverette is the only entrance and exit from the vehicle.**

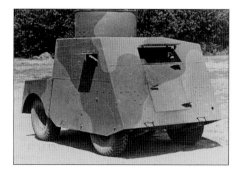

Beaverette IV Light Reconnaissance Car	🇬🇧

Country: UK
Entered service: 1940
Crew: 3
Weight: 2,540kg/2.5 tons
Dimensions: Length – 3.1m/10ft 2in
　　Height – 2.03m/6ft 8in
　　Width – 1.78m/5ft 10in
Armament: Main – 7.7mm/0.303in Bren light
　　machine-gun
　　Secondary – None
Armour: Maximum – 10mm/0.394in
Powerplant: Standard 14 4-cylinder 34kW/45bhp
　　petrol engine
Performance: Speed – 65kph/40mph
　　Range – Not known

Bedford Cockatrice

The Cockatrice was a mobile flame-thrower developed in 1940 by the Lagonda Company for airfield defence, using a Commer armoured truck as the prototype. The first production vehicles that came into service in early 1941 were built for the Royal Navy to act as airfield defence vehicles. Sixty of these vehicles were built using the Bedford QL 4x4 chassis. The armoured body was of a riveted construction, with the driver and engine at the front, the flame gun mounted in a small turret on the roof of the vehicle, and a machine-gun position at the rear with twin Vickers K guns. The flame projector used 36.4 litres/8 gallons of fuel per minute and had a range of 91.4m/300ft. The RAF were also looking at this type of vehicle but felt it was too small so asked for a vehicle to be developed based on the RAF's heavy fuel bowser which had an AEC 6x6 chassis. These were known as Heavy Cockatrice but only six of these vehicles were ever produced.

LEFT: **The Bedford Cockatrice has a very high ground clearance, with the flame gun mounted in the middle of the roof of the vehicle. The machine-gun position at the rear of the vehicle was open-topped.**

Bedford Cockatrice	
Country: UK	
Entered service: 1941	
Crew: 3	
Weight: N/A	
Dimensions: Length – 5.94m/19ft 6in	
Height – 2.59m/8ft 6in	
Width – 2.26m/7ft 5in	
Armament: Main – Flame Gun	
Secondary – 2 x Vickers K machine-guns	
Armour: Maximum – 11mm/0.43in	
Powerplant: Bedford 6-cylinder 53.7kW/72hp petrol engine	
Performance: Speed – 48kph/30mph	
Range – 370km/230 miles	

Bison Concrete Armoured Vehicle

Designed by Concrete Ltd which developed and built the vehicle, the Bison was a solution to the shortage of armoured vehicles in Britain in 1940. No two vehicles were the same, as any truck that could be scavenged was converted.

Leyland Lynx Bison	
Country: UK	
Entered service: 1940	
Crew: 5–10 men	
Weight: Variable	
Dimensions: Length – 6.1m/20ft	
Height – 2.74m/9ft	
Width – 2.28m/7ft 6in	
Armament: Main – Various small arms	
Secondary – None	
Armour: Maximum – 152mm/6in reinforced concrete, backed by 25mm/1in timber	
Powerplant: Leyland 6-cylinder 57kW/77hp petrol engine	
Performance: Speed – Variable	
Range – Variable	

The chassis were mainly pre-war civilian heavy trucks such as AEC, Dennis, Leyland, and Thorneycroft. The vehicle was covered in wooden shuttering and fast-setting concrete was then poured over it to a depth of 152mm/6in, which made it bullet-proof and capable of withstanding hits from guns of up to 37mm/1.46in. There were two main variations. The first had a concrete-covered engine and cab with a separate pillbox mounted on the flatbed. The engine and cab were open-topped but protected by canvas covers as concrete tops would be too heavy. The second type had the whole flatbed and driver's cab covered in concrete, with no openings in the sides or top. Access was by a trapdoor under

ABOVE: **The Bison driver and vehicle commander have a very limited vision from the cab. The wheels and chassis were very exposed and there was no protection below the vehicle. As a result of this, these vehicles were mainly used as static armoured pillboxes.**

the vehicle. These vehicles carried a crew of between five and ten men and had a variety of armament, the heaviest being an LMG (light machine-gun).

LEFT: **One of the final type of Birch Gun. Only two of these turreted vehicles were made. The turret has a high front and is really a barbette. This affected the elevation and maximum range of the gun.**
BELOW: **The four Mk II Birch Guns of 20 Battery Royal Artillery during an exercise on Salisbury plain. The Birch Gun was the first genuine self-propelled artillery. However, the gun shield on the vehicle gives the crew very little protection.**

Birch Gun

The Birch Gun was named after the Master General of the Ordnance, General Sir Noel Birch. Officially known as the SP QF (quick-firing) 18pdr Mk I, this was the first self-propelled gun to go into production for the British Army. The vehicle used many of the parts from the Dragon Carrier and the Vickers Medium tank.

The first gun entered service in January 1925 and was attached to 28 Battery, 9th Field Brigade, but only one of this early type was built and it was used for trials. The vehicle was fitted with an Armstrong Siddeley air-cooled engine, which gave it a top speed of 24.1kph/ 15mph but when used cross-country the maximum speed of the vehicle fell to 16.1kph/10mph. The vehicle was open-topped and there was no protection for the crew from the weather or from small

arms fire. The gun was mounted on a pintle mount towards the front of the vehicle which gave it a 360-degree traverse and a maximum elevation of 90 degrees so it could be used in an anti-aircraft role. It had a very complex sighting system and the recuperator was fitted to the top of the barrel.

Late in 1925 an order was placed with Vickers for four more Birch Guns, but these had a number of improvements to both the gun and the sighting equipment. The recuperator was moved to underneath the gun barrel and a gun shield was mounted on the front of the gun to give the crew some protection. These vehicles were issued to the 20th Battery of the 9th Field Brigade.

The third and final type of Birch Gun was ordered in December 1927 and was finished a year later but never issued. This model was equipped with a turret to give the gun crew some form of protection but this limited the maximum elevation and the range of the weapon.

The Birch Guns were used in the Experimental Mechanised Force manoeuvres of 1928, but by 1931 they had all been removed from service and the British Army would not get an SPG for another 11 years.

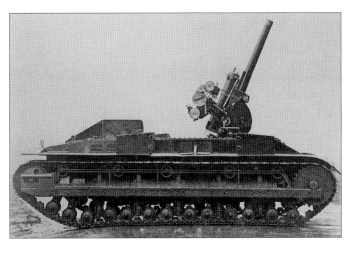

LEFT: **The prototype Birch Gun showing the 18pdr at full elevation. The vehicle was given the designation of Mounting SP QF (quick-firing) 18pdr Mk I, but was better known as the Birch Gun.**

Birch Gun	

Country: UK
Entered service: 1925
Crew: 6
Weight: 12,192kg/12 tons
Dimensions: Length – 5.8m/19ft
　Height – 2.3m/7ft 6in
　Width – 2.4m/7ft 9in
Armament: Main – QF (quick-firing) 8.17kg/18pdr
　Mk I gun
　Secondary – Small arms
Armour: None
Powerplant: Armstrong Siddeley 8-cylinder
　67kW/90hp petrol engine
Performance: Speed – 45kph/28mph
　Range – 192km/119 miles

Bishop 25pdr Self-Propelled Gun Mk 1

The successful use of self-propelled artillery by the German Army in the Western Desert led to urgent calls from the British 8th Army for something similar. It was suggested that the 25pdr gun could be mounted on a tank chassis and the best one for the job at this time was the Valentine. The Birmingham Carriage and Wagon Company were given the task of making this idea work in June 1941. A pilot model was ready for trials by August and an order for 100 vehicles was placed in November 1941.

The chassis was a basic Valentine Mk II tank with the standard turret replaced by a very large fixed box turret mounting a 25pdr gun. This gave the vehicle a very high silhouette, which was a great disadvantage in the desert. The gun could not be used to its maximum

elevation or range and so the vehicle was confined to the close-support role. Two large doors were mounted in the rear of the turret, which had to be open when firing the gun to give the crew extra room. The vehicle would often pull a 25pdr limber behind it for increased ammunition supply as it could only carry 32 rounds internally.

In early 1942, the British Tank Mission to America had seen a demonstration of the M7 and placed orders for it that March. However, production continued on the Bishop (the Royal Artillery gave its SPGs ecclesiastical names) and by July 1942, 80 of the first order had been built and a number had been shipped to the 8th Army in North Africa. As the last 20 were under construction, a further order for 50 was placed with the promise of an

order for 200 to follow, but this was cancelled in favour of the M7.

By July 1942 the M7 was entering service with the British and would be used alongside the Bishop for another year. The 8th Army used the Bishop until the end of the campaign in Sicily when it was replaced with the M7 and relegated to the training role. Compared to the M7, the Bishop was crude and unsophisticated.

ABOVE LEFT: **The crew of a Bishop have come out of action. Before they can rest, they have to tend to the vehicle by refuelling, rearming, checking the engine and all the other parts that make up the Bishop.**
ABOVE: **A Bishop driving off a raised bank. These banks were dug to help increase the range of the gun, with the vehicle commander helping to direct the driver.**

LEFT: **A group of British officers having an "O" (Orders) group, issuing orders for the next attack. The Bishop has been parked close to the trees to help camouflage it but the height of the fixed turret can be clearly seen. The vehicle is covered in personal kit.**

Bishop 25pdr SPG Mk 1

Country: UK
Entered service: 1942
Crew: 4
Weight: 20,320kg/20 tons
Dimensions: Length – 5.62m/18ft 6in
    Height – 3.05m/10ft
    Width – 2.77m/9ft 1in
Armament: Main – 25pdr (87.6mm/3.45in)
    gun howitzer
    Secondary – Small arms
Armour: Maximum – 60mm/2.36in
Powerplant: AEC 6-cylinder 98kW/131hp
    diesel engine
Performance: Speed – 24kph/15mph
    Range – 177km/110 miles

LEFT: **The mantlet has been covered by a canvas cover to help keep dust out of the gun mechanism and the pistol port has been opened on the side of the fighting compartment. The side-skirts are still attached to this Brummbär.**
ABOVE: **A knocked-out early Brummbär. The side skirt rails have been badly damaged. The vehicle is covered in** *Zimmerit* **paste to stop magnetic bombs being attached to the vehicle.**

Brummbär Sturmpanzer IV 15cm Self-Propelled Gun

As early as June 1941 a German Army paper suggested the idea of putting a 15cm/5.91in gun into an SP mount. In October 1942, Hitler was shown a plan drawn up by the firm Alkett for a close-support SPG using a 15cm short-barrelled gun mounted on the Panzer IV chassis. Hitler immediately insisted on the production of 40–60 of these vehicles, as he felt there would be a demand for them from the front-line troops, and on the development of a new high-explosive shell for the vehicle to use on buildings and other structures.

The first 60 vehicles were assembled by the Motor Vehicle Workshop in Vienna, the first 20 chassis being delivered in April 1943 with a further 32 in May. All were ready by June 1, 1943 and 50 were sent to Guderian on the Eastern Front, while 10 more were held back to be used at the Fuhrer's discretion. The Panzer IV Ausf F chassis required very little conversion: the turret was removed and a large box structure

was mounted on the top of the vehicle making it top-heavy. The frontal armour was increased to 100mm/3.94in and the driver's visor was at first the same as that in the Tiger 1, but later versions did away with this and replaced it with periscopes. At 28,651kg/28.2 tons, the vehicle was overloaded and the excessive weight caused suspension problems on the early vehicles, consequently the rubber-tyred wheels were replaced by steel-rimmed wheels on the first two bogie sets. Early service use showed that having no local defence machine-gun was a real handicap, so on later versions a machine-gun was mounted in the front of the hull above the driver. To increase the lower side protection for the vehicle, side plates called *Schürzen* (skirts) were hung from rails.

The Brummbär (Grizzly Bear) first saw action with *Sturmpanzerabteilung* 216 at Kursk, the largest tank battle of World War II, and later in Italy and in Normandy with units 217, 218 and 219.

ABOVE: **A late production Brummbär. The close-defence machine-gun port is mounted just above the driver's position on the front of the vehicle.**

Brummbär Sturmpanzer IV 15cm SPG

Country: Germany
Entered service: 1943
Crew: 5
Weight: 28,651kg/28.2 tons
Dimensions: Length – 5.93m/19ft 5in
　　Height – 2.52m/8ft 3in
　　Width – 2.88m/9ft 5in
Armament: Main – 1 x 15cm/5.91in StuH43 L/12
　　Secondary – 2 x 7.92mm/0.312in MG34
　　machine-gun
Armour: Maximum – 100mm/3.94in
Powerplant: Maybach HL 120 TRM 12-cylinder
　　petrol engine 223.7kW/300hp
Performance: Speed – 40kph/24mph
　　Range – 210km/130 miles

Buffalo LVT Amphibious Assault Vehicle

When the US Marine Corps were looking for a vehicle capable of landing troops or supplies from the sea in 1940, they saw a vehicle designed and constructed by a Donald Roebling who wanted a vehicle to use in the Florida Everglades. He called it the "Alligator". They liked it, asked for a few changes, and then placed an order for 300.

The LVT 1 (Landing Vehicle Tracked) could carry 18 fully armed men ashore or 2,041kg/4,500lb of stores. The vehicle was propelled through the water by its tracks as these had special oblique shoes that also gave it good traction on land. The driver's position was in the front of the vehicle with the engines mounted in the side walls of the cargo compartment. A big drawback was that the men in the rear of the vehicle

had to climb up the side of the vehicle and then drop 2.1m/7ft over the side on to the ground with a full combat load on their backs. Development of the LVT 1 was frozen in 1941 but as the vehicle was needed urgently by the Marine Corps, 1,225 of these vehicles were built in 1942. They were first used in action in August 1942 during the invasion of Guadalcanal.

Early in 1943 production started on the LVT 2, an improved version of the LVT 1. The general hull of the vehicle was redesigned and given a better boat shape to improve its water handling. The engines were removed from the sides and placed in the rear of the vehicle. The tracks were fitted with new track grousers that were W-shaped which could be easily attached to the tracks of the vehicle. Troops still had to climb the sides

ABOVE: **The rear ramp of this Buffalo LVT 4 is in the down position with a Weasel coming down the ramp. The grousers on the track, which move this very large vehicle through the water, can be clearly seen.**
LEFT: **A column of British Buffalos moving through the smokescreen to cross the Rhine in 1945. Some of the vehicles are still loading their infantry while the gunners of the leading Buffalo are getting their guns ready for action.**

and drop down on to the beach, which was causing casualties among the Marines, so a better way of debussing had to be developed. Two thousand nine hundred and sixty three of these vehicles were built and their first operation was the invasion of Tarawa in November 1943.

Production of the LVT 4, basically an improved LVT 2, began in December 1943. The improvements were that the engine was moved from the rear to the front just behind the driver. A ramp was now fitted to the rear of the vehicle, a major change that would turn this vehicle into the most successful amphibious assault vehicle of the war with 8,348 being produced. The ramp was operated by hand-winch in normal conditions, but in combat the ramp would be released to fall under its own weight. The rear cargo area could now carry 35 fully armed men, an artillery gun or a Jeep. The driver's position was moved from the middle of the driver's compartment to the right-hand side and a bow machine-gun was fitted for the second crewman to use. The first American operation for this vehicle was the invasion of Saipan in June 1944.

The LVT 3 was due to go into production in early 1944 but due to a number of design faults this was delayed until late 1944. Like the LVT 4 it had a rear cargo ramp, and two engines were mounted in the vehicle, one in each side sponson. Apart from the twin engines the LVT 3's performance was the same as the LVT 4, but its water handling was better than the other marks of LVTs. The Americans named the vehicle the

"Bushmaster". Two thousand nine hundred and sixty three of these were produced and it was used by the Marine Corps and the US Army for many years, taking part in the Korean War and serving into the Vietnam War. The first combat operation for the LVT 3 was Okinawa in April 1945.

The Buffalo, as it was called in British service, was assigned to the 79th Armoured Division. Four hundred and twenty five vehicles from two marks, the LVT 2 and the LVT 4, were sent over from America and these would take part in several river crossings. The first British operation using it was the assault on the Breskens Pocket in October 1944, and it remained in service with the British Army until the late 1950s.

ABOVE: **British Buffalos landing on Walcheren island at the top of the Scheldt estuary in 1944. The Buffalo was one of the few vehicles that could cope with the sand and mud of the island.** LEFT: **An LVT 1 driving at speed over swampy ground. These vehicles were nicknamed the "Swamp Angel". The very large driver's window is in the raised position. It gave the driver excellent vision but in combat was a weakness.**

Buffalo Mk IV/LVT 4

Country: USA
Entered service: 1942
Crew: 2 plus 35 infantry
Weight: 12,428kg/12.2 tons
Dimensions: Length – 7.95m/26ft 1in
    Height – 2.46m/8ft 1in
    Width – 3.25m/10ft 8in
Armament: Main – 1 x 12.7mm/0.5in machine-gun
    Secondary – 3 x 7.62mm/0.3in machine-guns
Armour: Maximum – 13mm/0.51in
Powerplant: Continental W670-9A 7-cylinder
    air-cooled radial engine 186kW/250hp
Performance: Speed – Land 32kph/20mph;
    Water 12kph/7mph
    Range – 240km/150 miles

LEFT: **A column of Bren Gun Carriers, No.2, Mk 1, escorting soft-skin troop transports. The hood over the aperture for the Bren gun was to make room for the weapon's magazine. The driver has his seat in the raised position and is peering over the top to see where he is going.**

Carriers – Machine-gun

A great deal of development was carried out by Vickers Armstrong during the early part of the 1930s using the Carden-Loyd light tank as the base vehicle. A new suspension system was developed consisting of a two-wheel Horstmann type unit with a large coiled spring each side and a single wheel unit behind. The idler wheel was at the front with the drive sprocket at the rear. The first vehicle was a machine-gun carrier. This had the driver on the right and the gunner on the left. Behind them there was room for four infantrymen to be

carried, though with very little protection. The first trials vehicle was produced in 1935 and a number of changes were made before 13 more were manufactured in 1936. A further order was placed later in 1936 for an extra 41 carriers. It was decided that three more types of carrier would be developed during 1936.

A carrier was developed to transport the 7.7mm/0.303in Bren light machine-gun forward under fire, as the gun was just coming into service. When that point was reached, this weapon could be used either from the carrier or dismounted. A number of these Bren Gun Carriers were still in service during World War II and saw action in the desert with the British 8th Army.

The Carrier Cavalry Mk 1 and the Scout Mk 1 were developed for the new

MIDDLE LEFT: **A pair of Carriers, Scout Mk 1. These vehicles had a crew of three and were armed with a Boys anti-tank rifle and a Bren gun.**

LEFT: **A group of four Bren Gun Carriers. The crew positions can be clearly seen, especially the third crew position behind the gunner. The suspension on each side has two road wheels in a Horstmann-type bogie which is sprung on coiled springs, a single wheel in a similar unit and the idler at the front.**

role that the mechanized cavalry units would carry out. The Carrier Cavalry had a driver and gunner in the front with seats on the rear for six cavalrymen, three each side sitting back-to-back. The first contract for 50 vehicles was placed in 1937. A large number of these carriers went with the BEF to France in 1940 but their original role was soon abandoned as it was too dangerous for the troops on the rear of the vehicle.

The Carrier Scout, of which 667 were built, carried various weapons and a radio mounted in the rear of the vehicle. Often confused with the Universal Carrier, it would see action with the BEF in France and in the desert.

Bren Gun Carrier	

Country: UK
Entered service: 1937
Crew: 3
Weight: 4,064kg/4 tons
Dimensions: Length – 3.66m/12ft
   Height – 1.37m/4ft 6in
   Width – 2.11m/6ft 11in
Armament: Main – Bren 7.7mm/0.303in
   light machine-gun
   Secondary – Small arms
Armour: Maximum – 12mm/0.47in
Powerplant: Ford 48kW/65hp petrol engine
Performance: Speed – 48kph/30mph
   Range – 258km/160 miles

LEFT: **The heavy turret bolts stand out clearly on this Cromwell. The tank is covered in personal storage.**
ABOVE: **The crew of this vehicle have rigged up a rain shelter above their map boards. They are wearing the one-piece tank-suit, which was very warm.**

Cromwell Command/OP Tank

This was the simplest and yet one of the most important conversions of World War II. Due to the speed and danger of a modern mobile battlefield, forward commanders required an armoured vehicle that was capable of keeping up with the advance units, yet giving them some protection and the fullest possible access to communications relevant to their task. These vehicles were issued to formation commanders and forward observation officers of the Royal Artillery.

The Cromwell was chosen due to its good speed and reliability, although at first there were a number of problems with the engine. The speed and power was supplied by a Meteor V12 engine that was a development of the Rolls-Royce Merlin aircraft engine. The top speed was initially 61kph/38mph but this was too much for the vehicle chassis to take, so the engine had a governor placed on it that reduced the speed to 52kph/32mph. From the outside, the vehicle would look very much like a conventional tank except for two map stands mounted on the top and towards the front of the turret. Inside the turret the whole main gun and its controls were removed, along with all the ammunition storage. The main gun barrel was replaced with either an aluminium or wooden copy to disguise the true purpose and configuration of this tank. This gave a lot of additional space for the extra radios that the vehicle carried. Three radios were placed in the turret area, two No.19 sets and one T43 Command radio set. In some vehicles, the Command radios were replaced by a ground-to-air radio set. In addition, two-man portable sets were carried for use by the Observation officers when away from the vehicle. The radios would be operated and maintained by members of the Royal Corps of Signals.

Three marks of Cromwell were converted to Command and OP tanks, these being the Mk IV, VI and VIII. These vehicles were to see service mainly in north-west Europe, and would remain in British Army service for many years after World War II.

Cromwell Command Tank

Country: UK
Entered service: 1944
Crew: 4/5
Weight: 26,416kg/26 tons
Dimensions: Length – 6.35m/20ft 10in
   Height – 2.5m/8ft 2in
   Width – 2.92m/9ft 7in
Armament: Main – None
   Secondary – 1 x Besa 7.92mm/0.312in
   machine-gun, and 1 x Bren 7.7mm/0.303in
   light machine-gun
Armour: Maximum – 76mm/2.99in
Powerplant: Rolls-Royce Meteor 12-cylinder
   447kW/600hp petrol engine
Performance: Speed – 52kph/32mph
   Range – 278km/173 miles

LEFT: **Two Cromwell Command tanks lead a column of Sherman tanks along a road. The map boards can be clearly seen on both Command tanks. The vehicles are clear of any personal clutter as they are on exercise in Britain.**

Crossley Armoured Car

In 1923, Crossley Motors of Manchester offered a new chassis that was very robust and cheaper than the Rolls-Royce, the main armoured car chassis used at this time. The Crossley six-wheeled chassis was used to produce a number of different armoured cars for the Royal Air Force (RAF) in the Middle East, the British Army in India, and a number of other governments in the 1930s.

The main contractor for building these vehicles was Vickers, which was able to build 100 six-wheeled armoured cars, most going to the British forces in India and Iraq. The first ones were based on the Crossley 30/70hp medium chassis and were over 6.1m/20ft long, so had a real problem with grounding in rough terrain. To overcome this problem Vickers mounted the spare wheels between the front and rear wheels so they hung below the chassis and could rotate freely, thus making it a four-axle vehicle which could withstand the rigours of less than perfect roads in the outlying

areas of India and Iraq. Another chassis was the 38/110hp Crossley IGA4 series with a six-cylinder engine. The body and turret were very similar to the Lanchester armoured car, but the turret was fitted with a single machine-gun. The Crossley 20/60hp light six-wheeled chassis was the basis for yet another armoured car. The first Crossleys were ordered from the Royal Ordnance Factory in 1928 and were armed with two machine-guns, one in a turret and one in the front hull. The turret was the same as a Vickers Mk 1 light tank.

Vickers produced a number of Crossley cars for export to several countries such as Argentina, Iraq and Japan. Most of these would see service for many years. The Iraqi cars were later commandeered by British forces and used by them in a training role until the

ABOVE LEFT: **Crossley armoured car on the 38/110hp chassis. This was known as the IGA4 series. The main customer for this car was the RAF.** ABOVE: **A Crossley 30/70hp chassis armoured car. The dome-shaped turret is very similar to the Indian Pattern armoured car and is armed with two Vickers guns.**

end of World War II. All Crossley cars in RAF service were equipped with ground-to-ground and ground-to-air radio sets. This proved very useful during combined operations in Iraq and India while trying to police the northern borders of these countries.

LEFT: **The pole frame above the vehicle carries the main aerial for the long-range radio, and for ground-to-air radio. The spare wheels were left free to rotate and so help the vehicle unditch itself.**

Crossley Mk 1 Armoured Car	

Country: UK
Entered service: 1931
Crew: 4
Weight: 5,516.88kg/5.43 tons
Dimensions: Length – 4.65m/15ft 3in
  Height – 2.64m/8ft 8in
  Width – 1.88m/6ft 2in
Armament: Main – 2 x Vickers 7.7mm/0.303in machine-guns
  Secondary – None
Armour: Maximum – 10mm/0.394in
Powerplant: Crossley 52kW/70hp
Performance: Speed – 80kph/50mph
  Range – 290km/180 miles

LEFT: **A Daimler armoured car opening fire in support of some infantry. This is not the normal role for this car as the main gun only fired solid shot.** BELOW: **The top hatch in the Daimler Mk 1 armoured car turret slides to the rear of the vehicle. A side hatch is situated between the wheels and storage boxes.**

Daimler Armoured Car

The Daimler Dingo was such a success that it was suggested that it could be scaled up into a wheeled tank. Development started in 1939 but due to a number of technical problems the armoured car did not enter service (as the Daimler Mk 1) until 1941.

The Daimler had many unusual and very advanced features for its time. There was no chassis to the vehicle and all the suspension components were attached directly to the armoured lower hull. Instead of a normal clutch, a fluid flywheel torque converter was used and also a pre-selector gearbox was fitted. The car had two driving positions, one in the front for the vehicle driver and one in the rear, which the vehicle commander could use to drive the vehicle away in reverse. The vehicle could use all five forward gears in reverse and was also

fitted with disc brakes some 20 years before any commercial vehicle. The turret mounted a 2pdr (40mm) gun. This was the first time that this gun was mounted in a British armoured car and was the same as that fitted to the Tetrarch light tank. The three-man crew meant that the vehicle commander had to act as loader for this weapon. Smoke dischargers were often fitted to the sides of the turret and some of the Mk 1 cars had a Littlejohn Adaptor fitted to their main armament. This was a squeeze bore muzzle adaptor that allowed the Daimler to achieve better armour penetration of enemy vehicles.

The Mk 2 came into service in 1943 with a number of improvements, including an improved gun mounting. The radiator was given better protection

and improved to give better engine cooling, and the driver was given an escape hatch. Apart from these modifications, the Mk 2 was the same as the Mk 1. Total production was 2,694 vehicles of all marks.

The Daimler soon developed a very good reputation for performance and reliability with the 8th Army in North Africa and it went on to serve with British forces in northern Europe. It remained in service until well after the end of World War II.

Daimler Mk 1 Armoured Car	

Country: UK
Entered service: 1941
Crew: 3
Weight: 7,620kg/7.5 tons
Dimensions: Length – 3.96m/13ft
　　　　Height – 2.24m/7ft 4in
　　　　Width – 2.44m/8ft
Armament: Main – 2pdr (40mm) gun
　　　　Secondary – Besa 7.92mm/0.312in machine-gun
Armour: Maximum – 16mm/0.63in
Powerplant: Daimler 6-cylinder petrol engine, 71kW/95hp
Performance: Speed – 80.5kph/50mph
　　　　Range – 330km/205 miles

RIGHT: **A post-World War II Daimler Mk 1. A spare wheel has replaced the storage boxes on the side of the vehicle. This vehicle is shown in desert camouflage as used by the 7th Armoured Division in 1942.**

Daimler Dingo Scout Car

One of the requirements for the new armoured force that was being developed in the late 1930s was for a light 4x4 scout car for general duties and reconnaissance. The design was originally put forward by the BSA motorcycle company, but they were taken over by the Daimler car company. An order for 172 vehicles was placed with the new company in 1939.

The Mk 1 was a 4x4 open-top vehicle which only had armoured protection for the crew at the front of the vehicle and proved to be under-powered. The Mk 1A incorporated all-round armoured protection for the crew and a bigger and more powerful engine. It also had a folding metal roof. These Mk 1 vehicles had four-wheel

steering and this proved to be a liability in the hands of unskilled drivers.

The steering was changed to be front wheels only in the Mk 2, which made it considerably easier to handle. The basic layout would hardly change during the course of the vehicle's production. The two crew members sat side by side in an open-topped armoured box, while the crew compartment had only a folding metal roof for protection. The engine was at the rear.

The Mk 3 was the heaviest version of the scout car but was still well within the limits of the vehicle. The metal roof was done away with as it was hardly ever used operationally by the crews. The engine was also given a waterproof ignition system.

ABOVE LEFT: **This Dingo Mk 1 is in the "buttoned down" mode with all the hatches closed. The rear view mirror is mounted on the top of the front plate but was rarely fitted.** ABOVE: **The frame on the back of the Daimler is to support the crew compartment hatch. The front part of the hatch folds back, and then both parts slide back and on to the frame.**

The vehicle was armed with a Bren gun for all of its service history although there were a number of local crew modifications on the armament. The Daimler scout car proved to be a very reliable and rugged vehicle and has the distinction of being one of the few vehicles to be in service at the start of the World War II and to remain in service well after the war had finished, with 6,626 of all marks being produced. This car could be found in most British and Commonwealth units, even in units that were not supposed to have it on strength.

ABOVE: **A Dingo Mk 3 in the North African desert. The roof hatch has gone on this mark. The crew have increased the firepower of the car by adding a Vickers gun.**

Daimler Dingo Mk 3 Scout Car	

Country: UK
Entered service: 1939
Crew: 2
Weight: 3,215.2kg/3.2 tons
Dimensions: Length – 3.23m/10ft 5in
    Height – 1.5m/4ft 11in
    Width – 1.72m/5ft 8in
Armament: Main – Bren 7.7mm/0.303in
    light machine-gun
    Secondary – None
Armour: Maximum – 30mm/1.18in
Powerplant: Daimler 6-cylinder petrol engine
    41kW/55hp
Performance: Speed – 88.5kph/55mph
    Range – 322km/200 miles

LEFT: **The importance of the Dorchester can be seen here as it is under armed guard. Inside the rear door is storage for a Bren gun.** BELOW: **The canvas cover running along the side of the vehicle is a side awning that can be pulled out and supported by the steel frame stored on the side of the vehicle.**

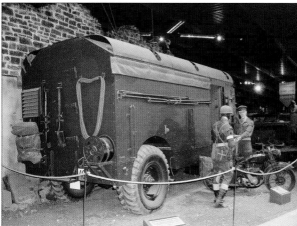

Dorchester Command Vehicle

The first command vehicle in British service was the Morris 762kg/ 15cwt. This came into service in 1937 but was far too small to be of any real use. The next vehicle was the 4x4 Guy Lizard which entered service in 1940 and most unusually had a Gardner diesel engine but again proved to be on the small side.

The Dorchester Command Vehicle was based on the AEC Matador chassis but with a few modifications. The fuel tank was moved and the winch was replaced with a generator for the radio sets that were carried in the vehicle. Two different marks of vehicle were produced, but there were no external differences between them – the changes were made to the internal fit

of the vehicle. The Mk 1 had a large single combined office and radio room, while in the Mk 2 there was a separate radio room. There were also two versions of each mark: the LP (Low Power) and HP (High Power) versions. The LP was fitted with No.19 radio LP and HP sets. The HP vehicle was fitted with an RCA (Radio Crystalline Amplifier) receiver and a No.19 set. The early versions of the vehicle were fitted with a canopy that, when unrolled, had side panels attached to form an extended working area. Later versions had a complete tent carried on the vehicle. There was normally a crew of seven with the vehicle, one driver, two radio operators and four officers.

Three Dorchesters were captured by the *Afrika Korps* in July 1941 and two

were given to Rommel to use as his own HQ vehicles. The official German designation for these vehicles was *Mammute* (Mammoths). The two vehicles used by Rommel were called "Max" and "Moritz" and were not recaptured by the British until the surrender of the German and Italian forces in Tunisia.

A new and larger vehicle did enter production towards the end of the war on the AEC 6x6 chassis. In all, 380 4x4 Dorchester command vehicles were produced from 1941–45. They would see service in North Africa, up through Italy and also in northern Europe.

LEFT: **The open side door of the vehicle has a blackout curtain on the inside, which was a standard fit. There is storage for several chairs on the back of the door. This door also gives access to the radio area and the driver's cab.**

Dorchester Armoured Command Vehicle	

Country: UK
Entered service: 1941
Crew: 7
Weight: 10,500kg/10.33 tons
Dimensions: Length – 6.32m/20ft 9in
　　Height – 3.1m/10ft 2in
　　Width – 2.4m/7ft 10in
Armament: Main – Bren 7.7mm/0.303in light
　　machine-gun
　　Secondary – None
Armour: Maximum – 12mm/0.47in
Powerplant: AEC 6-cylinder 71kW/95hp
　　diesel engine
Performance: Speed – 58kph/36mph
　　Range – 579km/360 miles

Dragon Carrier Mk I

A number of experimental vehicles were designed at the Tank Design and Experimental Department commanded by Colonel P. H. Johnson. The origins of the Dragon lay in a number of experimental tropical tanks that were supply vehicles. The fourth vehicle of this series was sent to the 9th Field Brigade in 1922 for trials in gun-haulage. The army were not very impressed with these

and so approached Vickers to produce three rival vehicles. One of these was built as a gun carrier for the 18pdr, the gun being carried on the top of the vehicle. It was hauled up ramps from the rear of the vehicle and positioned inside with the muzzle facing forward.

In 1922, the Royal Ordnance Factory at Woolwich produced two new vehicles called Artillery Transporters, which would

LEFT: **Light Dragon Carrier Mk IIc. This was an improved vehicle having a new suspension system designed by Horstmann. The vehicle exhaust on the rear of the body has been fitted with a shield. The external shields for the return rollers can also be clearly seen as can the canvas roof for the vehicle which is in the raised position.**

be the prototypes for the Dragon Mk I. One was sent to India for trials and the other was sent to the 9th Field Brigade. An order was placed for 20 vehicles, 18 for the army and two for the RAF, and these entered service in 1923. The driver's compartment was down in the front of the vehicle next to the radiator. The vehicle commander sat next to the driver high up on the top of the vehicle and behind them was seating for a further 10 men who would man the gun. The crew compartment on the top of the vehicle was completely open to the elements, but a canvas tilt could be placed over the crew to protect them from rain. At the rear of the vehicle was storage for ammunition.

As soon as they were issued, the 9th Field Brigade began training with their new vehicles. In July 1923, they took part in a long-distance road march from Deepcut to Larkhill, a distance of 93km/58 miles. The march was completed in just 10 hours and all the crews arrived in good order. A horse-drawn battery would only have been able to cover 20 miles in the same time. However, the Dragon had a number of mechanical problems and was withdrawn from service in 1926.

ABOVE MIDDLE AND ABOVE: **A Dragon Carrier with the roof folded to the rear of the vehicle, but it could also be collapsed and stored on one side. The carrier is shown with an 18pdr gun and limber, its normal load. Note that the gun and limber are still fitted with wooden wheels.**

Dragon Carrier Mk I

Country: UK
Entered service: 1923
Crew: 2 plus 10 gun crew
Weight: 9,144kg/9 tons
Dimensions: Length – 5.03m/16ft 6in
    Height – 2.13m/7ft – with tilt 3.05m/10ft
    Width – 2.74m/9ft
Armament: Main – None
    Secondary – Small arms
Armour: None
Powerplant: Leyland 6-cylinder 45kW/60hp
    petrol engine
Performance: Speed – 19kph/12mph
    Range – 145km/90 miles

LEFT: **This is the armoured version of the Model T. The armoured body of the vehicle is very narrow at the front and just fits around the engine and the driver. The door for the cab is accessed from the rear of the vehicle.**
BELOW: **A spare wheel is carried on the roof of the driver's cab. The machine-gun is mounted low in the rear of the vehicle, and had a very limited field of fire as it could not fire forwards due to the driver's cab.**

Ford Model T Scout Car

The Model T proved to be an outstanding scout and light armoured car, remaining in action long after other larger and more powerful armoured cars had broken down. There were two types of car built. The most numerous type used the basic Model T and was employed as a scout car. This was deployed mainly in the Middle East in countries such as Egypt and Palestine. The other type of car was a fully armoured version of the Model T and was used mostly in Russia and the Caucasus.

The scout car had a crew of two or three. In most of these, the machine-gun was mounted in the front of the car with the gunner sitting next to the driver. In some versions, a heavy machine-gun was mounted on the flatbed at the rear of the car. These vehicles had no armoured protection for the crew and no protection from the weather, while the machine-gun had very little traverse and none to the

rear. Nevertheless, due to its light weight and good reliability this vehicle proved to be well-liked by the men who used it. The American Army used several in Mexico and the Australians used them in Palestine and in Australia as they proved very good at covering large areas of dry, dusty ground.

The second car was developed by the British for the war in Russia, and designed by the Royal Navy, which had considerable experience with armoured cars. These vehicles were to replace a number of Lanchester armoured cars that had been damaged en route to Russia as they were all that was available at the time. Armour plate was placed around the engine and rear flatbed. The driver's cab was armoured except for the top which was canvas covered, and the Maxim machine-gun was mounted on a pintle mount on the rear flatbed with a 9mm/0.354in armoured shield fitted to it.

There was no forward field of fire for the machine-gun due to the driver's cab. These cars were ridiculed on arrival in Russia but soon proved far better than expected in service.

Ford Model T Scout Car	
Country: USA	
Entered service: 1914	
Crew: 2	
Weight: 508kg/10cwt	
Dimensions: Length – 3.42m/11ft 3in	
Height – 1.54m/5ft 1in	
Width – 1.28m/4ft 4in	
Armament: Main – 7.7mm/0.303in Vickers Maxim machine-gun	
Secondary – Small arms	
Armour: Maximum – 5mm/0.2in	
Powerplant: Ford 4-cylinder 16kW/22hp petrol engine	
Performance: Speed – 50kph/31mph	
Range – 241km/150 miles	

Grille 15cm Heavy Infantry Self-Propelled Gun Ausf M

By 1942 there was a growing demand for self-propelled artillery from the German Army so a number of chassis were considered for the task. The PzKpfw 38(t) was proving to be a very reliable and adaptable chassis and was used for a number of different gun platforms.

Development started in late 1942, and the prototype produced by Alkett using the 38(t) Ausf H chassis passed its acceptance trials. An order was placed for 200 units to be built on the Ausf K chassis, but this new chassis was not ready at that point, so construction started using the Ausf H. Production commenced in February 1943. After the initial production run was finished, it was agreed that all 38(t) chassis returned for repair could also be converted into SPGs. Some of them were adapted to become the Grille, in which a 15cm/5.91in sIG 33 was mounted across the top of the body of the vehicle and bolted into place and an armoured superstructure was placed around the vehicle. This also covered the engine area to accommodate ammunition storage.

As soon as it became available, the Ausf M chassis was used for the bulk of the production of the Grille, which finished in September 1944. This new vehicle had a number of changes made to it. The rear engine in the H was moved forward to a mid position and the fighting compartment was moved to the rear of the vehicle. To protect the fighting compartment, a large spring-loaded flap was used to cover the gun aperture when the gun was elevated.

Both versions of the Grille only carried 18 rounds of ammunition, so a further version was developed into an ammunition carrier using the Ausf M chassis. This was basically the same as the gun vehicle but without the gun, and consequently could be converted into the gun variant very quickly if needed. These vehicles were to see combat in Russia, Italy and northern Europe with many Panzer units of the German Army and the SS. In February 1945, there were still 173 Grille SPGs listed for combat.

Grille 15cm Heavy Infantry SPG Ausf M

Country: Germany
Entered service: 1943
Crew: 4
Weight: 12,192kg/12 tons
Dimensions: Length – 4.95m/16ft 3in
    Height – 2.47m/8ft 1in
    Width – 2.15m/7ft 1in
Armament: Main – 15cm/5.91in sIG 33/2
    Secondary – 7.92mm/0.312in MG34
    machine-gun
Armour: Maximum – 15mm/0.59in
Powerplant: Praga AC 6-cylinder 111kW/150hp
    petrol engine
Performance: Speed – 42kph/26mph
    Range – 190km/118 miles

LEFT: **A battery of Grille 15cm SPGs. The vehicle in the front of the picture is a late production variant, with the fighting compartment in the rear. The gun is at maximum elevation. When the weapon is in this position, a spring-loaded flap closes the gap in the gun shield.**

Guy Armoured Car Mk 1/1A

LEFT: **The driver's front hatch is in the open position, which improves the driver's vision. There are side hatches into the main fighting compartment just behind the front wheels on both sides. The very angular body and low ground clearance can be clearly seen.**

Following trials in 1938, the Guy Quad-Ant chassis was chosen to be the base for a "wheeled tank" as it was originally called. It was the first 4x4 vehicle to be specifically produced for the British Army. The engine was moved to the rear of the new vehicle, with a turret in the middle and the driver at the front. The other revolutionary thing about this vehicle is that it was of an all-welded construction for the hull and turret instead of riveted as specified for all other British AFVs at this time. An order was placed for 101 vehicles, one prototype and the remainder operational. The first 50 of these had one Vickers 12.7mm/0.5in and one 7.7mm/0.303in machine-gun. The next 50 vehicles had one Besa 15mm/0.59in gun and one 7.92mm/0.312in machine-gun. This configuration became the Mk 1A Guy Armoured Car. Only six of these went to France with the BEF and the rest remained in Britain with the Defence Force. All drawings were subsequently handed over to the Rootes Group.

Guy Armoured Car Mk 1/1A

Country: UK
Entered service: 1939
Crew: 3
Weight: 5,283kg/5.2 tons
Dimensions: Length – 4.12m/13ft 6in
 Height – 2.29m/7ft 6in
 Width – 2.06m/6ft 9in
Armament: Main – 12.7mm/0.5in Vickers
 machine-gun (Mk 1A 15mm/0.59in
 Besa machine-gun)
 Secondary – 7.7mm/0.303in Vickers machine-
 gun (Mk 1A 7.92mm/0.312in Besa machine-gun)
Armour: Maximum – 15mm/0.59in
Powerplant: Meadows 40kW/53hp petrol engine
Performance: Speed – 64kph/40mph
 Range – 338km/210 miles

Guy Lizard Command Vehicle

Britain appears to be the only country to develop and use the armoured command vehicle during World War II. There was a clear requirement for a 4x4 command vehicle equipped with radio for use as a mobile headquarters. The development programme was awarded to Guy in 1939, as they had finished the development of a heavy armoured car for the War Office.

Guy used the new Lizard 3,048kg/3-ton 4x4 chassis that the company had just developed. It was powered by the Gardner diesel engine which was most unusual for military vehicles at this time. The prototype was basically an open box with the driver's position accessible from the command area at the rear. This would be modified in the AEC Dorchester command vehicles in which the driver's compartment was separated from the rest of the vehicle. The original contract was for 30 of these but only 21 appear to have been built.

The majority of these vehicles remained in Britain but some were sent to join the 8th Army and at least one was captured by the Italians.

RIGHT: **Very few pictures of these command vehicles exist due to their security classification. This vehicle has been pictured in a base workshop. The large number of roof hatches can be seen. The canvas roll on the side of the vehicle is a tent that can be used as an office.**

Guy Lizard Command Vehicle

Country: UK
Entered service: 1940
Crew: 6
Weight: 10,668kg/10.5 tons
Dimensions: Length – 6.48m/21ft 3in
 Height – 2.67m/8ft 9in
 Width – 2.44m/8ft
Armament: Main – Small arms
 Secondary – None
Armour: Maximum – 12mm/0.47in
Powerplant: Gardner 6-cylinder 71kW/95hp
 diesel engine
Performance: Speed – 56kph/35mph
 Range – 563km/350 miles

LEFT: **Humber Mk 4 armoured car armed with the American 37mm/1.46in gun. These vehicles belong to the 49th Division, the "Polar Bears", and are taking part in an exercise in Britain during 1944.**
ABOVE: **The angular design of the vehicle can be clearly seen along with its Guy heritage. The crew are leaving the vehicle by the turret hatches as these were easier to use than the hull doors.**

Humber Armoured Cars

The Humber was one of the most important British armoured cars of World War II, and the Rootes Group were to manufacture 5,400 of these, some 60 per cent of all British armoured cars used in that conflict. Rootes had taken over the design and development of the Guy Mk 1 and used the Karrier KT4 chassis, but Guy would continue to supply the turrets and hull as they had the special welding equipment. The new design was placed into production and renamed the Humber Mk 1, entering service with British forces in 1941.

The Humber had a short wheel base and even with this was not very manoeuvrable, which crews found frustrating at times. The Mk 1 was armed with one 15mm/0.59in and one 7.92mm/0.312in machine-gun and a total of 500

were built before it was replaced by the Mk 2. The improvements in the Mk 2 were confined to a better glacis plate at the front of the vehicle and improved radiator armour at the rear. The Mk 3 entered production in early 1942 and had a new type of turret that increased the crew to four men. A number of Mk 3 cars were converted into mobile artillery observation vehicles. The Mk 4 reverted to a crew of three and now mounted the American 37mm/1.46in gun in the turret as the main armament, becoming the first British armoured car to be fitted with this weapon. The driver was given a rear flap that he could open by a lever so that he could see when reversing or in an emergency.

The Canadians built 200 of these vehicles, calling them the Armoured Car

Mk 1 Fox 1, but the crews could not tell the difference except in armament. Another British version was the AA (anti-aircraft) Mk 1 armoured car, which came into service in 1943 but was decommissioned in 1944. The turret carried four 7.92mm/0.312in machine-guns.

The Humber began its service life in North Africa and then moved on up into Italy. The Mk 4 was to see extensive service in northern Europe. Some cars would remain in service with other countries until the early 1960s.

LEFT: **This Humber is leading a Dingo and a Jeep along a lane in northern France in 1944. The car is covered in additional personal storage and is armed with a 37mm/1.46in gun. The driver has fairly good forward vision when his front plate is raised.**

Humber Mk 2–4 Armoured Car	

Country: UK
Entered service: 1941
Crew: 3 (Mk 3 – Crew 4)
Weight: 7,213kg/7.1 tons
Dimensions: Length – 4.57m/15ft
    Height – 2.34m/7ft 10in
    Width – 2.18m/7ft 2in
Armament: Main – 1 x Besa 15mm/0.59in, and
    1 x coaxial Besa 7.92mm/0.312in machine-guns
    Secondary – Bren 7.7mm/0.303in light
    machine-gun
Armour: Maximum – 15mm/0.59in
Powerplant: Rootes 6-cylinder 67kW/95hp
    petrol engine
Performance: Speed – 72kph/45mph
    Range – 402km/250 miles

LEFT: **The eight wheels of the Panzer IV running gear can be clearly seen on this vehicle. It has the late production driver's position and radio operator's box structure, with improved forward vision.**

ABOVE: **The spacious fighting compartment can be seen here. The main gun is mounted on the top of the engine compartment. In action the crew have no protection from the weather.**

Hummel 15cm Heavy Self-Propelled Gun

Reports coming back from the Panzer Divisions showed a need for a heavy SPG on a fully tracked vehicle. It was originally intended to mount the 10.5cm/4.13in medium gun but experiments showed that the heavy sFH18 15cm/5.91in guns could be mounted on a tracked chassis. Development stated in July 1942 with Alkett doing the work, and by combining parts from the Panzer III and the Panzer IV a successful vehicle was developed. Nevertheless, as the Hummel had only limited traverse, this was an interim solution to the problem until an SPG with an all-round firing-arc such as the Waffenträger could be developed.

The prototype was shown to Hitler in October 1942 and was cleared for production, with the first 100 being ready by May 1943 and 666 built by late 1944. The vehicle was given the name of Hummel (Bumble Bee) and would remain in production for the rest of the war. The gun barrel on the early vehicle was fitted with a muzzle brake at first but this was soon discarded as unnecessary. Another early feature was the long finger of the driver's position protruding forward. To ease production this was changed to an enclosed cab going from side to side of the vehicle. The engine was moved from the rear of the chassis to just behind the driver. The box-shaped armoured fighting compartment was roomy but gave very little protection to the gun crew, being only 10mm/0.394in thick with no protection from the weather, so a number of crews fitted canvas covers to improve their conditions. As it could only carry 18 rounds of ammunition, 157 Hummel vehicles were converted into ammunition carriers. With their gun apertures plated over, they could carry 40 rounds. The vehicle was popular with both its crews and the unit commanders as it gave them a mobile heavy punch against enemy targets.

The Hummel was first issued to units on the Eastern Front in early 1943 for the big push at Kursk which resulted in the largest tank battle in history and from then on would see action on every German front until the end of World War II.

RIGHT: **Due to the size of the vehicle, crews tried to camouflage them with netting which was tied to the sides of the fighting compartment. The rear doors are covered in personal kit that has been moved from under the gun.**

Hummel 15cm Heavy SPG

Country: Germany
Entered service: 1943
Crew: 6
Weight: 24,384kg/24 tons
Dimensions: Length – 7.17m/23ft 6in
    Height – 2.81m/9ft 3in
    Width – 2.87m/9ft 5in
Armament: Main – 15cm/5.91in sFH18/1 L/30
    Secondary – 1 x 7.92mm/0.312in machine-gun
Armour: Maximum – 30mm/1.18in
Powerplant: Maybach V-12 198kW/265hp petrol engine
Performance: Speed – 42kph/26mph
    Range – 215km/134 miles

Indian Pattern Armoured Cars

Shortly after the outbreak of World War I, arrangements were made in India to form an armoured car unit for internal security duties and for work on the North West Frontier. A number of these cars were built on any available chassis at the East Indian Railway Workshops at Lillooah. More vehicles were required as the Indian armoured car units expanded and chassis used included Minerva, Quad and even Fiat trucks. These were very basic armoured cars, even by the standards of the early RNAS vehicles.

Improved vehicles were sought in the 1920s. The first chassis used were the Rolls-Royce Silver Ghost but these were very expensive and Vickers looked for a cheaper alternative after only 18 vehicles. Crossley Motors of Manchester were able to provide a good strong chassis at half the price of Rolls-Royce and production of a 4x2 armoured car, using a Crossley truck chassis, started in 1923. The armoured car had the engine located in the front and the fighting compartment in the middle of the vehicle, topped by a domed turret which had four machine-gun mountings but only carried two guns. On the top of the turret was a small observation dome, and on some vehicles a searchlight was fitted to the top of this. The inside of the vehicle was covered in a thick layer of asbestos which helped insulate the crew from the heat of India. The insulation also served to protect the crew from an electrical charge, as the crew could electrify the hull exterior when any enemy climbed on to the car. The footbrake acted directly on the propeller shaft of the vehicle and consequently made the car somewhat skittish on slippery roads. The vehicle was fitted with solid tyres and firm suspension, so the ride for the crew was very hard.

The chassis of these cars were worn out by 1939, but the bodies were still in good condition, so the Chevrolet truck chassis was used to refurbish the vehicle. These cars would remain in service until Indian independence in 1947. The new vehicle was also sent to Palestine and Syria in 1940.

TOP: **A pair of Vickers armoured cars built on the Crossley chassis outside the Erith plant in Kent. On the top of the turret is a fixed searchlight.**

ABOVE: **A group of three Crossley armoured cars, one of which has been unable to stop. These vehicles are fitted with solid tyres, so that they operate in the rough terrain of India.**

Indian Pattern Crossley Armoured Car

Country: India
Entered service: 1923
Crew: 4
Weight: 5,080kg/5 tons
Dimensions: Length – 5.03m/16ft 6in
Height – 2.16m/7ft 1in
Width – 1.83m/6ft
Armament: Main – 2 x 7.7mm/0.303in machine-guns
Secondary – Small arms
Armour: Maximum – 8mm/0.315in
Powerplant: Crossley 6-cylinder 37kW/50hp petrol engine
Performance: Speed – 65kph/40mph
Range – 200km/125 miles

ABOVE: **An Indian Pattern Crossley car in Africa crossing a river by pontoon ferry. This armoured car has been fitted with aerials for a command radio set.**

LEFT: **The IS II tank chassis can be clearly seen on this vehicle. The drums fitted to the rear are extended-range fuel tanks. The thickness of the gun mantlet is 160mm/6.3in. On the roof of the fighting compartment is the DShK 12.7mm/0.5in machine-gun mount. A number of these vehicles were captured and pressed into German service.**

ISU-152mm Heavy Assault Gun

The first chassis used for this vehicle was the KV-1S, at which point it was called the SU-152. It was developed and placed into production in just one month. The first vehicles were rushed to the Kursk salient as the Russians knew the Germans were going to attack at this point. The SU-152 used the 152mm/5.98in M-1937/43 howitzer mounted in a heavily armoured box on the front of the vehicle. At this stage of the war the Red Army made no difference between anti-tank and other SPGs, so the howitzer was used in the anti-tank role and relied on the weight of the shell to knock out the German tanks.

The new tank project called the IS (Josef Vissarionovich Stalin) was initiated and the gun tank developed from this was placed into production in December 1943,

followed very quickly by the ISU-152. The same chassis was also fitted with the 122mm/4.8in M-1931/44 gun and this became the ISU-122. No muzzle brake was fitted on the end of the barrel, which also had a screw breech. The vehicle could carry 30 rounds of main armament ammunition. A later model, the ISU-122A, was developed using the 122mm/4.8in 1943 model cannon (D-25-S) which was a tank destroyer of exceptional size and power. This had a large double-baffle muzzle brake and had a higher muzzle velocity than the 152mm/5.98in gun.

The ISU-152 had one weakness and this was that the vehicle could only carry 20 rounds of ammunition, but no armoured ammunition carrier was available. Extra ammunition was brought

up to the ISU-152 by basic open truck, but the risk involved in this was considered acceptable as the ISU was such an important vehicle to the Soviet infantry and armoured forces.

Each tank brigade would have 65 ISU-152s attached to it, which would take part in every major battle from Kursk to the fall of Berlin. These heavy assault guns would be in the vanguard of the Soviet Army entering Berlin in 1945 and would remain in service until early 1970 with the Soviet forces.

LEFT: **This is one of the early SU-152 SPGs which has been knocked out by the Germans during the fighting at Kursk. The chassis is the KV heavy tank chassis.**

ISU-152mm Heavy Assault Gun

Country: USSR
Entered service: 1944
Crew: 5
Weight: 46,228kg/45.5 tons
Dimensions: Length – 9.05m/29ft 8in
　　　Height – 2.48m/8ft 2in
　　　Width – 3.07m/10ft 1in
Armament: Main – 152mm/5.98in M-1937/43 howitzer
　　　Secondary – 12.7mm/0.5in DShK 1938/43 AA machine-gun
Armour: Maximum – 90mm/3.54in
Powerplant: 12-cylinder W-2-IS 388kW/520hp diesel engine
Performance: Speed – 37kph/23mph
　　　Range – 180km/112 miles

LEFT: **Developed in 1944 for operations behind the German lines in France by the Special Air Service (SAS), the driver and gunner have bullet-proof screens in front of them and extra large fuel tanks in the rear of the Jeep.** BELOW: **This is one of the last batch of Jeeps to be converted for the LRDG. It has been fitted with a twin and a single Vickers K guns plus a single 12.7mm/50cal heavy machine-gun. The vehicle is covered in extra fuel and water cans.**

Jeep Multi-Role Vehicle

The Jeep is the best known vehicle of World War II. Easily adapted into a light AFV, its reputation has gone from strength to strength and is as great today as it was in 1940. In the late 1930s, the US Army held a series of trials to find a new command and reconnaissance vehicle. The trials that were held in 1940 were won by the Bantam Car Company, their competitors being Willys Overland and the Ford Motor Company. All the companies were given small construction orders in 1940, but in July 1941 the contract for 16,000 vehicles was placed with Willys. It soon became very clear that Willys could not keep up with demand so the US Army insisted that they pass over the drawings and other details to Ford so they could also produce this vehicle. Between them, these two companies built 639,245 Jeeps between 1941 and 1945, but as the vehicle was developed in the post-World War II years, other companies would produce this remarkable little vehicle. By 1962, when American production finished, 800,000 of these ugly little vehicles had been built.

The Willys MB was the standard Jeep of World War II, and the first unit to turn the Jeep into an AFV was the British Long Range Desert Group (LRDG). These men began by liberating several Vickers K machine-guns from the RAF stores in Cairo and mounting them on their Jeeps and other vehicles. Most Jeeps were fitted with twin Vickers machine-guns in the front and twin Vickers machine-guns on a pedestal mount in the rear, while every third Jeep would have a 12.7mm/50cal heavy machine-gun fitted. The fuel tank was also doubled in size to 136 litres/30 gallons, and a condenser was fitted in the front of the radiator. The Jeep was often used by officers as a light reconnaissance vehicle in the desert campaign as it had a good turn of speed and was very small. The Jeep was still further modified by the men in the field and great assortments of weapons of various calibres were mounted on the vehicle during the war in the desert.

LEFT: **British paratroopers leaving the Horsa glider landing zone on D-Day, June 6, 1944. The Jeep is pulling a light trailer full of ammunition, and eight men have managed to get on the vehicle. The Jeep has no armament fitted to it.**

LEFT: **Lt Colonel David Stirling and some of the men from the LRDG. He found the Jeep ideal for long-range missions behind enemy lines. The vehicles are heavily overloaded with extra fuel, water and ammunition.** ABOVE: **This American Jeep is fitted with twelve 120mm/4.72in rockets. These vehicles had a crew of two. The man inside the vehicle is operating the elevation gear. The crew area has been protected by an armoured cover.**

Airborne forces were also looking at the Jeep as a light AFV that could be fitted into gliders and yet on landing could supply a fast moving, heavily armed vehicle to hit the enemy hard and to act as a reconnaissance unit, as the special Jeep squadrons did at Arnhem. The US 82nd Airborne trapped at Bastogne added armour plate to their Jeeps and mounted either one or two 12.7mm/50cal machine-guns on them. These vehicles had a crew of six men and acted as a mobile "fire brigade" that would move around the defensive perimeter from one hot spot to another. Other conversions produced in Europe were the mounting of twelve 114.3mm/4.5in rocket tubes on the back of the Jeep by the 7th US Army. The cab was covered with armour to protect the vehicle.

The US Marine Corps would also adapt the Jeep into a light AFV by placing 28 M8A2 rockets on the rear thus turning it into a rocket artillery support vehicle. However, the crew could not remain with the Jeep when firing as it was too dangerous. Others would have multiple machine-guns fitted as these

vehicles could get into the jungle better than heavier tanks and LVTs. In 1944 the Americans undertook a trial with the T19 105mm/4.13in recoilless rifle, turning the Jeep into an anti-tank weapons platform. This was a pointer to the future.

After World War II the Jeep was developed and became the Willys MC, and by 1950 the M38 was entering service and would be used alongside the Willys MB in Korea. In 1960 Ford started to produce the last version – the M151. This and the M38 would see extensive service in Vietnam and with the Israeli Defence Forces during the Arab-Israeli wars of the 1960s and 1970s. The M151, better known as the "Mutt", was withdrawn from service with the US forces due to its nasty habit of turning over. Now armed with TOW anti-tank guided missiles, the Jeep is very much a modern tank killer, but still carries a number of machine-guns for close support. The Jeep has proved over time to be a real multi-role vehicle but is now being replaced in service by the Humvee; however, it has attained cult status with private military vehicle collectors.

LEFT: **An American captain using the direct sighting device for the 120mm/4.72in rockets. This is the prototype vehicle and has only been fitted with six rockets. These vehicles carried no reload missiles, which were carried in a supply truck. These vehicles proved very popular as they could deliver a big punch close to the front line.**

Jeep MR LRDG Vehicle

Country: USA
Entered service: 1941
Crew: 3
Weight: 2,540kg/2.5 tons
Dimensions: Length – 3.33m/11ft
    Height – 1.14m/3ft 9in
    Width – 1.57m/5ft 2in
Armament: Main – 2 x twin Vickers K
    7.7mm/0.303in machine-guns
    Secondary – Bren 7.7mm/0.303in light
    machine-gun
Armour: None
Powerplant: Willys 441 or 442 Go Devil 4-cylinder
    45kW/60hp petrol engine
Performance: Speed – 104kph/65mph
    Range – 900km/559 miles

LEFT: **Side view of the Ram Kangaroo, clearly showing the forward storage boxes built into the hull of the vehicle. The running-gear on this vehicle is very similar to that on the Grant Mk 3 tank.**
ABOVE: **A Canadian Ram Kangaroo of the 79th Armoured Division. The driver's forward hatch is in the open position, and next to it is the close-defence machine-gun turret. There are storage boxes built into the front mudguards.**

Kangaroo Armoured Infantry Carrier

Just after D-Day, the Canadian II Corps deployed Priest SPGs with their guns removed as infantry carriers in Normandy. Each of these vehicles could carry 12 men, but there were problems with their height so the Canadians looked for a better alternative. They had been using the Ram tank as a training vehicle in Britain before being equipped with the Sherman, so some 500 tanks were sitting idle. The Canadians moved these to their base workshop in France, which was codenamed "Kangaroo", where they were converted into armoured infantry carriers. The turret, ammunition bins and any other unnecessary bits were removed and two bench seats fitted in the open turret space.

The Ram was built in Canada using many of the parts from the American M3 tank. The Ram Mk II versions had an auxiliary machine-gun turret in the front of the vehicle that would be retained in the Kangaroo for close support and self-defence. Some later versions did not have this turret but a standard Sherman hull machine-gun. These vehicles were standard British right-hand drive with either the auxiliary turret or bow machine-gun on the left. Debussing was a problem because the troops were exposed as they jumped down from the top of the vehicle. However, the worst problem was getting the men into the vehicle, so very quickly climbing rungs were welded to the sides as a field modification. The infantry could not use their weapons from the vehicle and there was no overhead protection for the troops once inside. In addition to its infantry carrier role, the Kangaroo was also used for bringing forward ammunition, fuel and other supplies to troops under fire.

The Ram Kangaroo entered service piecemeal with the Canadians in September 1944 but in December 1944, these minor units were combined to become the 1st Canadian Armoured Carrier Regiment, joining up with the British 49th Armoured Personnel Carrier Regiment, which came under the command of the 79th Armoured Division. The first operation for the Ram Kangaroo was the assault on Le Havre – the last one was taking the 7th Infantry Division into Hamburg on May 3, 1945.

LEFT: **A Ram Kangaroo loaded with troops, moving through the Low Countries, 1944. The rear of the vehicle is covered with personal kit. The lack of any climbing ladders on the curved cast hull shows why the Kangaroo was difficult to climb into in full kit.**

Ram Kangaroo Armoured Personnel Carrier	
Country: Canada	
Entered service: 1944	
Crew: 2 plus 10 infantry	
Weight: 25,400kg/25 tons	
Dimensions: Length – 5.79m/19ft	
Height –1.91m/6ft 3in	
Width – 2.77m/9ft 1in	
Armament: Main – None	
Secondary – 7.7mm/0.303in Browning machine-gun	
Armour: Maximum – 60mm/2.36in	
Powerplant: Continental R-975 298kW/400hp petrol engine	
Performance: Speed – 40kph/25mph	
Range – 232km/144 miles	

LEFT: **A battery of Katyusha rocket vehicles being positioned for firing. The very simple M13 rockets were slid into position so that one rocket rides on the top of the rail while the other suspended on the same rail runs along the underneath.** ABOVE: **The 6x6 Studebaker chassis can clearly be seen along with the very basic rocket rail system. The armoured shield for the cab folds back on to the roof of the cab.**

Katyusha BM-13 132mm Rocket Launcher

The BM-13 rocket launcher was the first self-propelled artillery weapon produced in quantity by the Soviet Union. This system was given a number of cover names, one being Kostikov Guns, but was officially designated the Guards' Mortars. The popular nickname for the vehicle was "Katyusha", a diminutive form of Katerina, which was the title of a popular piece of music at the time.

Development started on the M-132 in 1938 and at first was not very successful, mainly because the rockets were fired over the side of the vehicle. The first chassis used was the ZiS-5 truck, and with the rocket rails now mounted longitudinally, it proved to be very successful and was placed on test in August 1939. Production started in 1940 with the Soviet Army designating the vehicle BM-13-16.

Several different truck chassis were used as rocket launchers for the Katyusha system, most of them lend-lease vehicles from Canada and the United States. The most common mount was the 2,540kg/2.5-ton 6x6 Studebaker truck of which over 100,000 had been sent to the Soviet Union. This vehicle was selected for its superior cross-country performance and reliability, with nearly 10,000 being converted into Katyusha. The Soviets used the chassis, engine and cab of the Studebaker, leaving the rear for the rocket rail system. The cab was covered in anti-blast armour that covered the windscreen to protect it from the rocket motor blast. The Studebaker and its Hercules JXD engine would be copied and built after World War II by the Soviet Union.

These vehicles were at first issued to special units under the control of the NKVD (Soviet Secret Police) with the first combat action taking place at Orsha in July 1941. It had a devastating effect on the average German soldier and was given the German nickname of "Stalin's Organ". The Soviets would mount several other types of rocket on the basic vehicle, the largest of these, the M-30 300mm/11.8in, entering service in 1944. The battle for Berlin in 1945 would see over 400 Katyusha batteries bombarding the Germans. This system finally left Soviet service in 1980.

LEFT: **The rear of the BM-13 showing the rear supporting jacks that were lowered when firing. The launching platform had very little traverse so the whole vehicle was aimed at the target.**

Katyusha BM-13 132mm Rocket Launcher

Country: USSR
Entered service: 1941
Crew: 4
Weight: 6,096kg/6 tons
Dimensions: Length – 7.47m/24ft 6in
   Height – 3.05m/10ft with rocket rails in
   the down position
   Width – 2.21m/7ft 3in
Armament: Main – 16 x 132mm/5.2in rockets
   Secondary – None
Armour: Maximum – 5mm/0.2in
Powerplant: Studebaker Hercules JXD 6-cylinder
   65kW/87hp petrol engine
Performance: Speed – 72kph/45mph
   Range – 370km/230 miles

Kfz 13/14 Medium Armoured Car

This was a medium 4x2 car based on the chassis of the Adler Standard 6 passenger car. In 1932 the German Army issued a requirement for this kind of vehicle, and after extensive trials it was placed into production in late 1933, entering service in 1934. Being inexpensive and simple to produce, it very quickly appeared in relatively large numbers, being issued to cavalry units as a reconnaissance vehicle.

The engine was mounted in the front with a 4-speed gear box which drove a conventional rear axle. The hull was box-shaped with an open top and all-welded construction. The Kfz 13 had the driver in the front, with the vehicle gunner and commander sitting in the rear. The machine-gun was pedestal mounted and had a limited traverse with the main field of fire to the front. There was no radio set in the vehicle, and consequently all communication was done by means of flags. The Kfz 14 was an unarmed radio car with a crew of three, with a large frame aerial mounted above the crew compartment that when not in use could be folded down flush with the top of the crew compartment. These vehicles were known popularly by their crews as "*badewannen*" (bath-tubs). Being two-wheel drive the vehicle had a poor cross-country ability, which was not helped by also having a high centre of gravity. The 8mm/0.315in armour plate also gave very little protection to the crew.

These vehicles were built as training and reconnaissance cars for the new German Army. Normally a section of Kfz 13 reconnaissance cars would operate alongside one Kfz 14 radio car. Both vehicles were due to be replaced by the Sd Kfz 221 by 1939, but war came too soon and a large number of both the Kfz 13 and the Kfz 14 were still in front-line service. They would see action in Poland, the invasion of the Low Countries and France during 1939–40. Some were still acting as reconnaissance vehicles for non-motorized infantry units during the invasion of Russia in 1941.

TOP: **A mixed column of Kfz 13 and 14 armoured cars moving along a road. The very high radio aerial frame can be clearly seen on the second car.**

ABOVE: **The very clean and simple design of the car is apparent, but the wheels of this vehicle were very easily damaged.**

LEFT: **The driver of this vehicle has his seat in the raised position so that he has good all-round vision. The gunner is in his normal position which is a little exposed.**

Kfz 13/14 Medium Armoured Car

Country: Germany
Entered service: 1934
Crew: 2 (Kfz 13) and 3 (Kfz 14)
Weight: 2,235.2kg/2.2 tons
Dimensions: Length – 4.17m/13ft 8in
　　Height – 1.45m/4ft 9in
　　Width – 1.68m/5ft 6in
Armament: Main – 7.92mm/0.312in MG13 machine-gun (Kfz 13)
　　Secondary – Small arms
Armour: Maximum – 8mm/0.315in
Powerplant: Adler 6-cylinder 45kW/60hp petrol engine
Performance: Speed – 70kph/44mph
　　Range – 300km/186 miles

LEFT: **A Lanchester of the RNAS with all the hatches in the open position. Additional water storage for the radiator has been fitted to the side of the engine. The wire wheels were standard fit for this car.** ABOVE: **The rear of a Lanchester armoured car with the rear doors open; this was the main entrance and exit for all the crew. This vehicle is operating in Russia and has been fitted with additional armour to protect the gun barrel.**

Lanchester Armoured Car

After the Rolls-Royce, the Lanchester was the most numerous type of armoured car produced by the British in World War I. Designed by the Admiralty Air Department for the RNAS Armoured Car Section operating in France, the prototype was produced in December 1914, using the Lanchester Sporting Forty touring car chassis, with production following in early 1915. A number of changes were made to the basic chassis, the main ones being that the suspension and chassis were strengthened to take the extra weight of the armour plate, and dual wheels were fitted to the rear axle to improve the vehicle handling. The Lanchester had sloping armour over the front and bonnet of the car and the engine was mounted

beside the driver. While the engine was powerful and very reliable, and also used an advanced epicyclic gearbox, the Lanchester could never get over the problem of the weak chassis that would be its Achilles' heel.

In 1915 the RNAS armoured cars were handed over to the army, which looked at the great variety of cars it had acquired and decided to standardize on the Rolls-Royce. This standardization would make resupply of spare parts much easier. The Lanchesters were all sent back to Britain for overhaul before being despatched to Russia with No.1 Squadron RNAS Armoured Car Division. The squadron arrived in Russia in 1916 and would remain there for a year fighting in Persia, Romania and Galicia,

and operating in climates ranging from desert to near-Arctic conditions. During their time in Russia these cars covered 85,295km/53,000 miles. The cars were deployed in a manner that would become the standard for AFV warfare in the 20th century. Acting as scouts and armed raiders, they operated well forward of the infantry following in their armoured trucks. When operating alongside the infantry, they would act as fire-support vehicles. Their final operation was as part of the unsuccessful Russian Brusilov Offensive of mid-1917. After this Russia descended into civil war and the RNAS Armoured Car Division was withdrawn back to Britain.

LEFT: **A Lanchester 6x6 Mk 1 armoured car. This was a vast improvement over the early 4x2 Lanchester. The new vehicle was armed with three machine-guns, two in the turret and one in the hull next to the driver.**

Lanchester Armoured Car	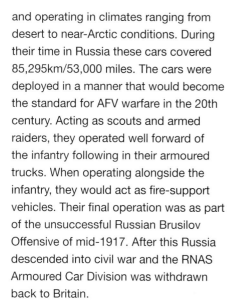

Country: UK
Entered service: 1915
Crew: 4
Weight: 4,876.8kg/4.8 tons
Dimensions: Length – 4.88m/16ft
   Height – 2.29m/7ft 6in
   Width – 1.93m/6ft 4in
Armament: Main – Vickers 7.7mm/0.303in
   machine-gun
   Secondary – 7.7mm/0.303in Lewis gun,
   and small arms
Armour: Maximum – 8mm/0.315in
Powerplant: Lanchester 6-cylinder 45kW/60hp
   petrol engine
Performance: Speed – 80kph/50mph
   Range – 290km/180 miles

LEFT: **A Loyd Carrier towing a 6pdr AT gun and carrying the whole crew waits to pass a German Panther tank. The vehicle is overloaded with ammunition and personal equipment.** ABOVE: **The drive-shaft of the vehicle is in a very exposed frontal position, but this made it easy to maintain. The front of the carrier is very clean and well sloped. This vehicle has the canvas weather protecting roof in the raised position.**

Loyd Carrier

The Loyd Carrier was developed by Captain Vivian Loyd in 1939 as a simple cross-country tracked vehicle, using many existing components from various vehicle manufacturers. The basic vehicle was based on the 762kg/15cwt 4x2 Fordson truck, with tracks and suspension from Vickers light tanks.

The carrier used a basic Ford engine, radiator, gearbox and transmission, with the engine and radiator being mounted in the rear of the vehicle. The power from the engine was brought forward to the front sprockets, with brakes fitted to the front and rear sprockets. Steering was by means of steering levers that applied the front and rear brakes on one side of the vehicle or the other depending on the direction of turn, but care had to be taken as a track could be easily broken or shed. The vehicle was a simple open box with access either side of the engine in the rear, or over the side to get into the driver's position. An order was placed with Captain Loyd's firm in late 1939 for 200 carriers.

Originally intended as an infantry carrier with a capacity of between eight and ten men, the Loyd was very quickly adapted into various specialist roles. This included mechanical cable laying for the Royal Signals units or as a starting vehicle for tank units, as the Loyd was fitted out as a battery slave unit that was capable of starting tanks or charging batteries. There were also several trials using the carrier as an SPG mount for the 2pdr anti-tank gun and the 25pdr gun howitzer. However, the Loyd was mainly produced and used as a towing vehicle with infantry battalions for the 6pdr (57mm) anti-tank gun and the 107mm/ 4.2in mortar. These carriers were simple to maintain in the field and well-liked by their crews. They were built by the Vivian Loyd Company until 1941 but as demand increased during World War II, production was undertaken by five different companies in several different countries with Ford as the main manufacturer. Some 26,000 vehicles of this type were constructed during the war. A very adaptable vehicle, it was found in all British theatres of war.

RIGHT: **The rear of a Loyd Carrier. The engine can be clearly seen in the middle of the vehicle and takes up most of the space. The carrier has a 6pdr gun attached to the hitch. The lack of storage space can also be seen, as four men were carried in this area.**

Loyd Carrier

Country: UK
Entered service: 1940
Crew: Various
Weight: 4,064kg/4 tons
Dimensions: Length – 4.14m/13ft 7in
　　　　Height – 1.42m/4ft 8in
　　　　Width – 2.06m/6ft 9in
Armament: Main – None
　　　　Secondary – Small arms
Armour: None
Powerplant: Ford 8-cylinder 63kW/85hp petrol engine
Performance: Speed – 48kph/30mph
　　　　Range – 193km/120 miles

Lorraine Schlepper 15cm Self-Propelled Gun

After the fall of France, the Germans captured a large number of AFVs from the French Army and at first placed them in storage. Among these were the Lorraine tractor units. The French had originally built 387 of these. The driver sat in the front, with the engine just behind and a large cargo area in the rear. Converting these vehicles into an SPG carriage was not difficult: the rear cargo area and suspension were strengthened to take the gun mount. The exact number of captured chassis is not known but over 300 were repaired and converted into self-propelled mounts as either an anti-tank weapon or gun howitzer.

In May 1942 the vehicle, armed with the 15cm/5.9in FH13, was demonstrated to Hitler who passed it for further conversion. Initially 60 chassis with 10.5cm/4.13in le FH18, 40 chassis with 15cm/5.9in FH13 and 60 armed with the PaK40 7.5cm/2.95in were converted. Each vehicle was fitted with an open-topped fighting compartment with the main weapon filling most of this area. Most crews fitted a canvas cover over the top that could be quickly removed when necessary. The superstructures were made by Alkett and shipped to Paris where they were fixed to the chassis and issued to German units in France. It was standard practice for captured vehicles to remain in German service in the country where they were

captured. The 15cm/5.9in vehicle had a recoil spade fitted to the rear to help stabilize the vehicle during firing. The armour of the fighting area was very poor and was only just shell-splinter proof.

In July 1942, the first of these conversions arrived in North Africa. Ten were issued to the 21st Panzer Division and eleven to the 15th Panzer Division, and these would take part in the German attack on El Alamein. By November 1942, all the initial batch of vehicles had been destroyed or captured by the British. Large numbers of these vehicles were still available by D-Day, June 6, 1944, when 131 of the PaK40 conversion, 54 of the 15cm/5.9in FH13 and 37 of the FH18 with the 10.5cm/4.13in gun were serviceable.

TOP: **A British Crusader tank towing a captured Lorraine Schlepper in the desert of North Africa. The small size of this SPG can be seen against the bulk of the tank.** ABOVE: **The rear of the Lorraine Schlepper showing the recoil spade in the raised position. When lowered into the ground, this helped to absorb some of the recoil from the gun.**

LEFT: **The diminutive size of the vehicle is clear in this picture. This allowed the vehicle to be easily hidden. The driver's position is below the gun barrel, with the engine immediately behind the driver.**

Lorraine Schlepper 15cm FH13 SPG

Country: Germany
Entered service: 1942
Crew: 5
Weight: 8,636kg/8.5 tons
Dimensions: Length – 5.31m/17ft 5in
  Height – 2.23m/7ft 4in
  Width – 1.83m/6ft
Armament: Main – 15cm/5.91in sFH13/1
  Secondary – 7.92mm/0.312in MG34 machine-gun
Armour: Maximum – 10mm/0.394in
Powerplant: Delahaye 6-cylinder 52kW/70hp petrol engine
Performance: Speed – 35kph/22mph
  Range – 135km/84 miles

LEFT: **An M3 with the bad-weather roof-cover in place. This vehicle is fitted with a "pulpit" machine-gun mount over the vehicle commander's position. The armoured shutter for the windscreen is in the "up" position and has been used as a storage shelf for personal kit. The large whip aerial has been pulled over and attached to the front of the vehicle.**

M3 Half-Track Infantry Carrier

The Americans bought two French Citroen-Kegresse half-tracks during 1925 and purchased a further one in 1931. After a number of developments, they married the White Scout Car with the Kegresse suspension and came up with what would become the classic American half-track of World War II. The Car Half-Track M2 and the M3 Carrier Personnel Half-Track were two of the first half-track vehicles produced by the Americans in that conflict. The M2 was designed as a reconnaissance vehicle and as a prime mover for guns of up to 155mm/6.1in, while the M3 was designed as a personnel carrier for armoured divisions and motorized artillery. The distinction between the two vehicles very quickly disappeared once committed to action. These models were approved for production in October 1940 and entered service in 1941 with the American Army.

Under the competitive bidding system of the US Ordnance Department, the lowest bidder is awarded the construction contract. The Autocar company won the bid and secured the construction contract, but was very quickly joined by Diamond T and White. Total production would be 12,499 M3 vehicles of all marks, while 11,415 M2 carriers of all marks were built. It was agreed by the three manufacturers that as many parts as possible would be interchangeable between the M2 and M3.

The M3 could carry 13 men: the driver, commander and co-driver in the front with 10 infantry behind. The back of the vehicle had five seats on each side looking into the middle, with a large door in the rear. The armour on the rear crew compartment was only 7mm/0.28in thick, while that on the cab doors, windscreen shutter and radiator grill was 12.7mm/0.5in.

ABOVE: **The gunner's "pulpit" can be clearly seen on this vehicle, which is carrying four machine-guns. The vehicle exterior is covered with personal kit as there is no room inside to store the equipment of the ten-man crew.**

Armament was very varied and a lot depended on the crew of the vehicle. Officially there were to be two machine-guns, a 12.7mm/50cal in the front and a 7.62mm/30cal in the rear on a pintle mount. On the outside of the vehicle down each side of the rear compartment were two racks for carrying 24 anti-personnel mines.

In 1943 the M3A1 was developed and went into production in October of that year. The main improvement was to the armament of the vehicle. A M49 ring mount was fitted over the co-driver's position to take a single 12.7mm/50cal machine-gun. In the rear, three pintle sockets were installed each mounting a 7.62mm/30cal machine-gun. Diamond T was the main contractor and 2,862 of these vehicles were built before the contract was cancelled in January 1944. The last M2 was built in March 1944, and the last M3 was produced in February 1944 as sufficient of this type were stockpiled.

The M3A2 which was due to replace the M2, M2A1, M3, and M3A1 was going to be a universal carrier with movable storage lockers inside the vehicle. Depending on the role, it could be able to carry between 5 and 12 personnel with a great variety of weapons. The vehicle was passed by the Armoured Board in October 1943, but was never placed into serious production.

Production of brand new vehicles might have ceased in early 1944, but vehicle modification was still going strong with 2,270 M3 carriers upgraded to M3A1 standard. Personnel kit storage was very poor in the vehicle as it was never designed to act as a home-from-home for the section of men who lived and fought from their vehicle. The crews would personalize their vehicles by welding extra storage racks on the outside, in particular on either side of the door at the rear. The racks for mines on the side of the vehicle were converted to carry boxes of food and other important personal items.

One extremely important characteristic of these half-tracks was that the crew could fight from the inside of the vehicle in some safety. As more tracked gun tractors became available the half-track was passed over to the infantry. These vehicles could be found in every Allied army during World War II and on every front. In 1980 the M2/M3 could still be found in service with 22 different armed forces and some of these vehicles can still be found in service with the Israeli Defence Force reserve units.

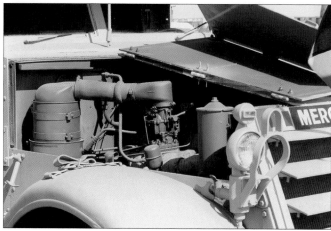

TOP: **The driver's cab in the M3 is relatively spacious and has a very simple layout. The driver and vehicle commander have very good vision from the cab of the vehicle, but it is roofless.** ABOVE: **Access to the engine of the M3 was very good and it was simple to work on or maintain. The armoured louvers of the radiator grill can be open or closed from the driver's position.**

LEFT AND BELOW LEFT: **The front of these vehicles are fitted with a winch. The rack on the side of the crew compartment was originally intended for the storage of landmines. These vehicles are fitted with only a single machine-gun.**

M3A1 Carrier Personnel Half-Track

Country: USA
Entered service: 1943
Crew: 3 plus 10 infantry
Weight: 10,160kg/10 tons
Dimensions: Length – 6.14m/20ft 3in
　　　　　　　Height – 2.69m/8ft 10in
　　　　　　　Width – 2.22m/7ft 3in
Armament: Main – 12.7mm/0.5in Browning
　　　　　　machine-gun
　　　　　　Secondary – 3 x 7.62mm/0.3in machine-guns
Armour: Maximum – 12.7mm/0.5in
Powerplant: White 160 AX 6-cylinder 95kW/128hp
　　　　　　　petrol engine
Performance: Speed – 64kph/45mph
　　　　　　　　Range – 280km/200 miles

M3A1 Scout Car

The forerunner of this car was designed in 1933 by White and was based on a 4x4 van chassis produced by their subsidiary Indiana. The prototype (T7) was an open-topped scout car, armed with two 12.7mm/50cal and two 7.62mm/30cal machine-guns, which carried a crew of four men. The vehicle was placed into production and was given the designation M1, with a total production of 76 cars.

The M2 followed in 1935. It was bigger and more powerful and could carry a crew of seven, but only 20 of these vehicles were produced. White went on to produce the M3 version of this scout car and had delivered 64 to the US Army by 1938. Marmon-Herrington

also produced a number of these scout cars for Iran.

The M3A1 entered service in 1940 and would remain in production until 1944, by which time some 20,856 scout cars had been built. Fast and very reliable, it was well-liked by its crews, but its cross-country performance was poor and it was soon replaced by the half-track for many tasks. To help improve its off-road capability a roller was fitted to the front of the car. The open fighting compartment was a serious weakness – the men were very exposed and the rear was a grenade trap. However, it was fitted with the Tourelle skate rail that allowed the machine-guns to give all-round fire. General Patton used one as a command vehicle but had additional armour fitted and raised around the fighting compartment. The M3A1E1 was developed to increase the range and fuel economy of the vehicle. This model was fitted with the 58kW/78hp Buda-Lanova diesel engine and had a speed of

ABOVE: **This British M3A1 Scout car belongs to the 11th Armoured Division and was photographed in Normandy in 1944. The front of the vehicle has been fitted with a wire-cutter pole, and has had its roller removed.**

87kph/54mph. All of these vehicles, the total production of which was 3,340, were sent to Russia.

Most of the M3 scout cars in British service were used in a secondary role, being issued to units like the engineers, signals and medical corps. Some of these vehicles were to remain in service with a number of countries after World War II, particularly the French.

M3A1 Scout Car

Country: USA
Entered service: 1940
Crew: 2 plus 6 infantry
Weight: 5,618kg/5.53 tons
Dimensions: Length – 5.62m/18ft 5in
   Height – 2m/6ft 6in
   Width – 2.03m/6ft 8in
Armament: Main – 12.7mm/0.5in Browning
   machine-gun
   Secondary – 2 x 7.62mm/0.3in Browning
   machine-guns
Armour: Maximum – 12.7mm/0.5in
Powerplant: White Hercules JXD 6-cylinder
   71kW/95hp petrol engine
Performance: Speed – 105kph/65mph
   Range – 400km/250 miles

LEFT: **The driver's cab has a very simple layout. The dashboard has just two instrument dials and five switches, while the vehicle commander has a glove box. The wiper motors are mounted above the windscreen.**

M3 75mm Gun Motor Carriage

The half-track served as the carrier for numerous self-propelled weapons, but relatively few of these would be standardized. The notable exception would be the anti-aircraft mounts that would remain in service for years after the end of World War II.

Development was started in June 1941 in response to a request from both the British and American armies for a mobile self-propelled anti-tank gun. The project was to mount the M1897 A4 75mm/2.95in gun in an M3 half-track. This gun was an American copy of the French 75mm/2.95in from World War I. The original gun mount was the M2A3, but there was a shortage of these and so the M2A2 was substituted on the M3A1 half-track conversion.

Autocar were given the first contract to convert these vehicles and built 86 in 1941. Fifty were sent to the Philippines to help bolster the forces there. Autocar produced a total of 2,202 of these conversions but due to a shortage of guns, 113 of these vehicles were converted back into personnel carriers.

A number of conversions were made to the basic carrier, these being the moving of the fuel tanks to the rear of the fighting compartment and adding a new sub-floor to the rear of the fighting compartment, along with storage for 59 rounds of 75mm/2.95in ammunition. Initially the vehicle crew was four but this was quickly increased to five. The gun shield at first allowed the gun crew to stand full height behind the gun but this gave the vehicle a high silhouette so it was made smaller. First used in the defence of the Philippines against the Japanese, the vehicle proved to be a very good gun platform. The next major operation it was used in was "Torch", the invasion of North Africa by the Allies in 1943. In British service, these vehicles were known as "75mm SP Autocar" and were used by HQ troops of armoured car reconnaissance units. Even after being declared obsolete in September 1944, they would remain in service with many units until the end of the war.

ABOVE: **A US Marine Corps vehicle is landed on a beach from an LCT (Landing Craft Tank). The vehicle has been fitted with three extra machine-guns. The front of the half-track has also been fitted with a winch, which proved very useful in the jungle fighting.**

ABOVE: **A battery of American half-tracks armed with 75mm/2.95in guns belonging to Patton's forces in Sicily. Most of the personal kit has been placed at the rear of the vehicle and on the ground.**

LEFT: **A line-up of five gun half-tracks at their training ground in the USA in 1942. All the vehicles have been fitted with the unditching roller.**

M3 75mm Gun Motor Carriage

Country: USA
Entered service: 1941
Crew: 5
Weight: 10,160kg/10 tons
Dimensions: Length – 6.14m/20ft 3in
　　　　　　Height – 2.26m/7ft 5in
　　　　　　Width – 2.22m/7ft 3in
Armament: Main – 75mm/2.95in M1897 A4
　　　　　Secondary – 7.62mm/0.3in machine-gun
Armour: Maximum – 12.7mm/0.5in
Powerplant: White 160 AX 6-cylinder 95kW/128hp petrol engine
Performance: Speed – 64kph/45mph
　　　　　　Range – 280km/200 miles

M5 Half-Track Personnel Carrier

Because demand was out-pacing production at the White Company factories building the M2 and M3, the M5 was built by the International Harvester Company (IHC). This new production facility started in April 1942 and produced 9,291 half-track carriers, most of them going to Lend-Lease. The M5 was similar in design to the M2 and M3 half-tracks, but their parts were not interchangeable as IHC used many of their own components in their vehicle. Obvious changes were the curved rear corners of the rear fighting compartment, the flat front mudguards and the use of homogeneous armour plate which increased the vehicle's weight.

The M5 entered service in December 1942 and remained in production until October 1943, when it was replaced by the M5A1. Like the M2A1 and the M3A1,

the improvement was in armament and the introduction of the M49 ring-mount. Between October and December 1943, 1,859 M5A1s were built, with a further extension to the contract of 1,100 vehicles with completion in March 1944. In April 1943 it was decided that IHC should produce a universal carrier to the same specification as the M2 and M3 carriers, but like these other universal carriers, the M5A2 was never put into production. The M5 itself would remain in production until June 1945.

The last version of this half-track was the M9A1 and this was the same as the M2A1. There was no basic version of the M9 as it was already fitted with the M49 ring-mount and the extra machine-gun mounts in the rear of the vehicle. Total production of the M9A1 was 3,433, with nearly all going into British service.

ABOVE LEFT AND ABOVE: **This M5 is covered in personal equipment, armed with three machine-guns and is fitted with a winch on the front of the vehicle. The shipping panel is still on this vehicle below the commander's door.**

Large numbers of M5 and M5A1 half-tracks were sent to the Soviet Union along with M17 anti-aircraft units. In British service, the M5 and the M9A1 were converted into several specialist roles such as radio and medical half-tracks. Other large users were the Royal Engineers (RE) and the Royal Electrical and Mechanical Engineers (REME). Large A-frames were fitted to the front so these vehicles could act as recovery vehicles in the field. They remained in British service until 1966.

LEFT: **Like the M3, the M5 was fitted with a storage rack for landmines but in combat it was never used for this purpose. The driver's side window is unglazed, having just a metal shutter with a very small vision slit cut in it.**

M5 Half-Track Personnel Carrier

Country: USA
Entered service: 1942
Crew: 3 plus 10 infantry
Weight: 10,668kg/10.5 tons
Dimensions: Length – 6.33m/20ft 9in
  Height – 2.31m/7ft 7in
  Width – 2.21m/7ft 3in
Armament: Main – 12.7mm/0.5in Browning
  machine-gun
  Secondary – 3 x 7.62mm/0.3in Browning
  machine-guns
Armour: Maximum – 10mm/0.394in
Powerplant: International Red 450B 6-cylinder
  107kW/143hp petrol engine
Performance: Speed – 61kph/38mph
  Range – 201km/125 miles

M8 Greyhound Light Armoured Car

Armoured cars have acted as the armed reconnaissance vehicle of the American Army for a long time. During 1940–41, the Americans were able to observe the war in Europe and study the new operational trends, and so develop a number of new vehicles. Four companies entered the competition for the new heavy armoured car, and in 1941 the Ford T22 was chosen for this role. It went into production in late 1942 with the first vehicles entering service in early 1943, but the 37mm/1.46in main gun was considered to be too small by 1942 for a "heavy" designation, so the new car was given the revised designation of Light Armoured Car. The M8 remained in production until 1945, by which time 8,523 vehicles had been built.

The M8 was a 6x6 lightweight vehicle of all-welded construction, with the driving compartment in the front, turret in the middle and engine at the rear. The turret had an open roof and was hand-operated by a crew of two, while the other two crew members occupied the driver's position in the front of the vehicle. It had excellent cross-country ability, a low silhouette, and plenty of room for the crew. One weakness was its thin floor armour, so most crews covered the floor with sandbags to help protect themselves against the blast of a mine.

A variation on the M8 was the M20, which was basically the same vehicle except that the turret was removed. The fighting compartment was also cut away and fitted with a ring-mount for a 12.7mm/50cal machine-gun. The M20 was used as a reconnaissance and supply vehicle, and some 3,791 were built.

A few M8s were supplied to the British but it was not liked, as the armour was considered to be too thin. In 1973, the French demonstrated a new version of the M8 armed with the H90 90mm/3.54in turret. Some 22 countries still operated the M8 in 1976, and the Brazilian Army fitted their M8 cars with guided AT missiles.

ABOVE: **The clean lines of this vehicle are very apparent as is the two-man turret. It is one of the prototypes, and as such has no personal kit stored on the car.** LEFT: **The roof hatches above the driver's and co-driver's positions are open and folded to the side. The headlights have a protective frame over them and the turret has been fitted with a heavy machine-gun.**

RIGHT: **The wheels and chassis of the M8 are well protected from damage by angled covers. The driver's and co-driver's hatches are fully closed and, as can be seen, the vision slits are small and making forward vision very limited. A tie-down rail is fitted around the middle of the turret.**

M8 Greyhound Light Armoured Car

Country: USA
Entered service: 1943
Crew: 4
Weight: 8,128kg/8 tons
Dimensions: Length – 5m/16ft 5in
    Height – 2.25m/7ft 5in
    Width – 2.54m/8ft 4in
Armament: Main – 37mm/1.46in gun M6,
    and coaxial 7.62mm/0.3in machine-gun
    Secondary – 12.7mm/0.5in machine-gun
Armour: Maximum – 19mm/0.75in
Powerplant: Hercules JXD 6-cylinder 82kW/110hp
    petrol engine
Performance: Speed – 89kph/55mph
    Range – 563km/350 miles

M8 75mm Howitzer Motor Carriage

The American Army made repeated requests for a close-support howitzer and these were met in early 1942 by the appearance of the T30 half-track howitzer. This was developed as an expedient project in 1941 and entered production very quickly, with some 500 contracted to be built. However, only 320 were actually produced. The vehicle used the M1A1 75mm/2.95in pack howitzer, mounting the weapon on a new tracked chassis that was just becoming available.

This new chassis was the M5 and the first test vehicle built was the T41 Howitzer Motor Carriage, in which the howitzer was mounted on the hull centreline.

The vehicle existed only as a mock-up and was abandoned in favour of a new design – the T47. This new vehicle, now named the M8, still used the M5 chassis, but this time the weapon, the M2 or M3 75mm/2.95in howitzer, was mounted in a rotating turret. The 75mm/2.95in turret was much larger than the M5 turret and so the hull had to be altered to fit it, with the driver's hatches moved forward on to the glacis plate. The M8 was fitted with two V8 Cadillac engines, and proved to be a reliable vehicle. A mock-up was produced in April 1942 and was approved, with production starting in September 1942. The total number of vehicles built was 1,778 with production finishing in January 1944.

As the M7, a 105mm/4.13in howitzer mounted on the Sherman chassis, began to appear in greater numbers, the M8 was replaced in armoured formations and passed to reconnaissance units to replace half-track mounted close-support weapons. The M8 was also passed on to the Free French forces and other Allied nations. In the Pacific, the M8 was used in the close-support role by the Marine Corps and was well-liked,

LEFT: **An M8 caught up in a traffic jam with a column of Jeeps. The turret of this vehicle is fitted with a manual traverse only, as it is an artillery vehicle and not a tank.**

ABOVE LEFT: **The large glacis plate on this vehicle is very striking, and has the driver's and co-driver's hatches recessed into it. Above these hatches each man has his own periscope.** ABOVE: **Two M8 SPGs are leading two half-tracks and a 2,540kg/2.5-ton truck down a road in Britain. In combat these vehicles would be covered in personal kit and tow an ammunition trailer.**

as it could bring a large weapon close to enemy positions to help extract them from caves and other dug-in positions. The M8 was often fitted with an ammunition trailer in the European theatre of operations as it only carried 46 rounds in the vehicle itself.

M8 75mm Howitzer Motor Carriage

Country: USA
Entered service: 1942
Crew: 4
Weight: 15,605kg/15.45 tons
Dimensions: Length – 4.41m/14ft 6in
　　　Height – 2.32m/7ft 7in
　　　Width – 2.24m/7ft 4in
Armament: Main – 75mm/2.95in M2 howitzer
　　　Secondary –12.7mm/0.5in Browning
　　　machine-gun
Armour: Maximum – 44mm/1.73in
Powerplant: 2 x Cadillac V8 series 42 82kW/110hp
　　　petrol engine
Performance: Speed – 56kph/35mph
　　　Range – 210km/130 miles

M12 155mm Gun Motor Carriage

The M12 was one of the earliest self-propelled mounts to be designed, but was one of the last weapons to enter active service in World War II. Development started in June 1941 with a test model being ready in February 1942. The vehicle was based on the M3 chassis and mounted a 155mm/6.1in gun, the M1918, an old French weapon used as a towed field gun by the Americans during World War I and then placed into storage as obsolete.

Originally this vehicle was rejected by the army as they could see no need for such a powerful weapon on a self-propelled mount. The army had plenty of towed guns which it felt would more than meet any future requirement. The Ordnance Department disagreed, feeling there was a specific need for this kind of piece, and ordered 50 vehicles in March 1942. This order was overruled by the

Supply Board until the vehicle had been fully tested by the Artillery Department. The Artillery Department reported back in agreement with the Ordnance Department that there was a need for the M12 and recommending that it should be placed into production. This started in late 1943, but for 100 vehicles only, and was completed in March 1944.

The vehicle had a two-man compartment at the front for the driver and the vehicle commander. The engine was in the middle of the vehicle just behind the driver's compartment with an open gun area at the rear. There was only room for 10 rounds of ammunition and so the rest of the crew travelled on the M30 supply vehicle, which was an M12 without the gun and its mounting carrying an additional 40 rounds of ammunition and the other four men of the gun crew under a canvas cover.

ABOVE LEFT: **An American battery of M12 vehicles has been placed into the sustained fire position. The guns have been driven up and on to a raised ramp which helps increase the elevation of the gun.**

ABOVE: **The open nature of the fighting compartment of this vehicle can clearly be seen. The travel lock for the gun barrel is lying on the glacis plate between the driver's and co-driver's position.**

June 1944 saw 74 of these vehicles arrive in Europe and they made a big difference instantly. They were used as "door knockers" by the Americans during their attacks on the Siegfried Line. One of these guns would be brought forward and the Germans inside the defensive position were offered the options of surrender or having their bunker blown apart around them.

LEFT: **An American M12 being readied to fire. The target cannot be far away as the gunner is checking the visual sight and the barrel is flat. The gun might be about to be used as a "door knocker" on a fixed-defence structure.**

M12 155mm Gun Motor Carriage

Country: USA
Entered service: 1944
Crew: 6
Weight: 29,464kg/29 tons
Dimensions: Length – 6.73m/22ft 1in
　　Height – 2.69m/8ft 10in
　　Width – 2.67m/8ft 9in
Armament: Main – 155mm/6.1in M1918M1 gun
　　Secondary – 12.7mm/0.5in Browning machine-gun
Armour: Maximum – 50mm/1.97in
Powerplant: Continental R-975 Radial
　　263kW/353hp petrol engine
Performance: Speed – 39kph/24mph
　　Range – 225km/140 miles

M40 155mm Gun Motor Carriage

At the end of 1943, the American Army decided to standardize their AFV chassis into the Light Weight Combat Team based on the M24 light tank, and the Medium Weight Combat Team based on the M4A3 Sherman tank. The main idea behind this was to make production, the supply of spares and servicing quicker and easier for the troops in the field. Development of this new weapon started in January 1944, following the decision to send the M12 to Europe. The American Army Armoured Force Board still firmly believed that they did not require the M40 but the success of the M12 in active service forced them to change their minds.

The M40 fell into the Medium Weight Combat Team, as it was designed around the M4A3 chassis. This was widened and Horizontal Volute Spring Suspension (HVSS) was fitted. The general layout was the same as the M12 with the driver located in a crew compartment in the front of the vehicle, the engine in the middle and the gun in the rear area. An escape hatch was also fitted into the floor of the driver's compartment just behind the co-driver's position. The fighting compartment was open, as in the M12, because this vehicle was never intended to be deployed in the front line but several miles behind supporting the front-line troops. Like the M12 there was a recoil spade

ABOVE: **The M40 used the same chassis as the M4A3 Sherman tank, which helped to make the supply of spares easier. The gun is fitted with a shield but this gives the gun crew very little protection. The travel-lock for the gun barrel is in the raised position.**

attached to the rear of the vehicle and operated by a hand winch. The M40 would carry a new gun, as supplies of the M1918 had finished, and this would be the 155mm/6.1in M1 or the 203mm/8in howitzer, both very successful towed weapons that had proved themselves in combat. In March 1944, five pilot models were ordered from the Pressed Steel Car Company, with production starting in February 1945 and not finishing until late 1945. Total production for the M40 was 418 vehicles. The upper hull was made of 12.7mm/0.5in homogeneous armour plate, but gave the crew no protection at all as the sides were too low. Development of an armoured cover for the crew area of the M40 was under way but with the ending of World War II, the need for this shelter also ended. The vehicle could not carry a lot of ammunition in the fighting compartment so it was intended to convert some as cargo carriers. These would carry extra ammunition and also the other crew members for the gun. They were never developed because there was a shortage of vehicle chassis as they were urgently needed in northern Europe.

The Americans had problems in breaching the concrete bunkers during the fighting along the Siegfried Line as they had no AFV that could do this, unlike the British who had developed the Churchill AVRE. They got over this by bringing up the M12 to point-blank range (732m/2,400ft), calling on the German defenders inside to surrender and if they failed to do so, then blasting the bunker open. Due to the success of the M12 in breaching these bunkers, a larger weapon was developed to go on the M40 chassis to be used as a siege gun. This carried a 250mm/9.84in short-range mortar, but development was stopped in August 1945 as the war had finished.

The M43, the vehicle carrying the 203mm/8in howitzer, was developed at the same time as the M40, but was not put into production until August 1945. An order for 576 of these weapons had been placed but by the cessation of hostilities, only 48 had been built before the order was cancelled.

The M40s arrived in Europe in time to take part in the final battles in Germany, their first action being the bombardment of Cologne. They would remain in service with the American Army until the late 1950s, having proved their worth during the Korean War. The British Army bought a number of M40 and M43 vehicles from the Americans after the war and these would remain in service until the early 1960s. The M40 proved to be a very reliable and well-liked vehicle, and the men who manned this weapon were known as "long-range snipers" due to the accuracy of the gun.

TOP AND ABOVE: **The driver's hatch was changed to an all-round vision cupola on the M40. There is a periscope through the top of the hatch. The lower picture shows the working end of the gun, the breach of which is an interrupted screw breach.**

ABOVE RIGHT: **Three fire extinguishers were attached to each side of the gun shield.**

ABOVE LEFT AND LEFT: **Inside the driver's position. The hand controls are in the middle of the picture with the foot pedals at the bottom. The recoil spade is in the lowered position and just requires the vehicle to reverse to push it into the ground.**

M40 155mm Gun Motor Carriage

Country: USA
Entered service: 1945
Crew: 8
Weight: 40,640kg/40 tons
Dimensions: Length – 9.04m/29ft 9in including gun barrel
Height – 2.69m/8ft 10in
Width – 3.15m/10ft 4in
Armament: Main – 155mm/6.1in M1A1 gun
Secondary – Small arms
Armour: Maximum – 12mm/0.47in
Powerplant: Continental 9-cylinder 295kW/395hp radial petrol engine
Performance: Speed – 38.6kph/24mph
Range – 161km/100 miles

LEFT: **One of the prototype vehicles on test at the Aberdeen Proving Ground in the USA. When they were used in the ground-support role these vehicles were called "Meat Choppers".**
BELOW: **The gun mount for the M16 is the M45D. The low height of this mount required the sides and back of the rear compartment to be capable of folding down.**

M16 Multiple Gun Motor Carriage

Development started in December 1942 on a new vehicle as a replacement for the M13 which mounted the under-powered twin 12.7mm/50cal M33 gun. The improved version, known as the M16, carried the M45 gun mount.

The White Motor Company started production of the M16 in May 1943 and continued until March 1944, with a total production of 2,877 vehicles. The gun mount was placed in the rear fighting area which had been cleared of all the internal fittings. The rear area had no rear door and the tops of the sides were hinged so the guns could fire over the sides and rear of the vehicle. The new turret for the M16 was fitted with four 12.7mm/50cal machine-guns and had to be raised by 152mm/6in so that the guns could clear the sides of the vehicle. The

M16 could carry enough ammunition for eight minutes firing of the M45 gun mount. White were also given a contract to convert 677 M13 vehicles up to M16 standard, while a further 60 vehicles were converted by Diebold Incorporated, bringing total production of the M16 to 3,614 vehicles in all.

The M17 was similar to the M16, the only difference being the chassis, for while the M16 used the M3, the M17 used the M5. International Harvester produced a total of 1,000 M17s between December 1943 and March 1944, and all were sent to the Soviet Union under the Lend-Lease programme.

The M16 would see service on most fronts during World War II. They proved extremely valuable to the Marines in the Pacific as they could bring a large amount of firepower into a concentrated area. These vehicles would remain in service with the American Army until 1958 but the M45 gun mount would

LEFT: **The M16 had very little storage room for ammunition so most of these vehicles had a small ammunition trailer which was pulled behind the vehicle. Some of these systems would remain in active service for 40 years.**

remain in service until 1970. The chassis had changed but the M45 would find widespread use during the Vietnam War mounted on M54 5,080kg/5-ton supply trucks. In 1980 these vehicles were still in service with 12 different countries.

M16 Multiple Gun Motor Carriage

Country: USA
Entered service: 1943
Crew: 5
Weight: 10,160kg/10 tons
Dimensions: Length – 6.14m/20ft 3in
   Height – 2.62m/8ft 7in
   Width – 2m/6ft 6in
Armament: Main – 4 x 12.7mm/0.5in Browning
   machine-guns
   Secondary – Small arms
Armour: Maximum – 12.7mm/0.5in
Powerplant: White 160AX 6-cylinder 95kW/128hp
   petrol engine
Performance: Speed – 64kph/45mph
   Range – 280km/200 miles

Marmon-Herrington Armoured Cars

South Africa had never produced an AFV until development started on the Marmon-Herrington armoured car. Progress was slow at first but once war was declared this speeded up dramatically. The chassis was made by Ford and imported from Canada, the four-wheel drive was imported from Marmon-Herrington in America and all the armament came from Britain. The armour plate was supplied by local factories and the assembly plants were old railway workshops.

The Mk 1 was only two-wheel drive and this was discovered to have poor cross-country ability. At first the vehicle had a riveted construction but this was quickly changed to an all-welded fabrication. Total production of the Mk 1 was 135 vehicles.

The Mk 2 was very similar in layout to the Mk 1 but was now fitted with four-wheel drive which improved its performance. The hull of the vehicle was quite spacious for the crew of four and had twin doors at the rear. The Mk 2 came in two variations: the Middle East (ME) and the Mobile Field Force (MFF). The ME had a Boys anti-tank rifle in the turret and two mounts on the turret for Bren guns, one being anti-aircraft. There were also flaps on each side of the vehicle for additional Bren guns. The MFF had a 7.7mm/0.303in Vickers machine-gun in the turret and another one in a ball mount on the near side of the vehicle. Total production of these vehicles was 549 MFF and 338 ME, and in the early days of the North African campaign they were the main armoured car used by British forces. A number of Mk 2s were converted with captured Italian and German weapons. The armour was a little thin so on the Mk 3 this was increased.

ABOVE LEFT: **This car has been fitted with a captured German 37mm/1.46in AT gun, which is mounted over the driver's position. A Vickers machine-gun is fitted in the rear.** ABOVE: **This column of cars is being prepared for a patrol in East Africa. Some of these cars have had additional Vickers machine-guns fitted to the rear of the turret.**

The Mk 2 was to see extensive service with British forces in several theatres of war. Some were even captured by the Japanese and used by them. Others were sent to East Africa and the West Indies. These cars were to prove surprisingly effective and easy to operate, with some remaining in service after the war.

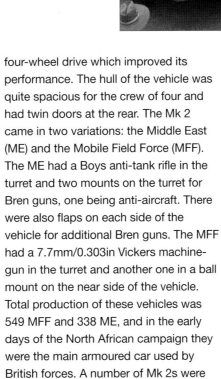

LEFT: **These Marmon cars have been fitted with different turrets. The first vehicle has a heavy and a light machine-gun in the turret, while the following cars have been fitted with a single machine-gun.**

Marmon-Herrington Mk 2 ME Armoured Car

Country: South Africa
Entered service: 1941
Crew: 4
Weight: 6,096kg/6 tons
Dimensions: Length – 5.18m/17ft
    Height – 2.67m/8ft 9in
    Width – 2m/6ft 6in
Armament: Main – Boys 14mm/0.55in
    anti-tank rifle
    Secondary – 2 x Bren 7.7mm/0.303in
    machine-guns
Armour: Maximum – 12mm/0.47in
Powerplant: Ford V8 63kW/85hp petrol engine
Performance: Speed – 80kph/50mph
    Range – 322km/200 miles

LEFT: **The first version of the Marder III was this vehicle, which is armed with the Soviet 76.2mm/3in gun. Both the high position of the gun and the very exposed crew position can be clearly seen. This was very much a makeshift vehicle with everything piled on top of the chassis. A total of 344 of these vehicles were produced between April and October 1942.**

Marder III Self-Propelled Anti-Tank Gun

The Marder, the German name for the marten – a vicious little animal of the weasel family, was a series of three different vehicles built on several different chassis. Production of all three variants started in 1942 with three different manufacturers and in three different countries. They would remain in active service with the German Army until the end of World War II.

The Marder I was built on the captured French Lorraine Schlepper using the PaK40 anti-tank gun as main armament. The conversions were undertaken by a factory in Paris and all vehicles were to be issued to German units based in France. The Germans had captured over 300 of these old vehicles, most of which were converted into self-propelled artillery, but 84 were converted into Marder I anti-tank vehicles. The fighting compartment was at the rear and was surrounded by a sloped superstructure. The PaK40 retained its own gun-shield as a

form of mantle, but the main weakness was the open top to the fighting compartment which was a serious grenade trap.

The Marder II was built on the chassis of the Panzer II, but the German Army was by now questioning whether or not the Panzer II was still capable of combat. The driver's compartment was at the front, the fighting compartment in the middle and the engine at the rear. The main armament was again the excellent PaK40 anti-tank gun. Production started in 1942 and finished in June 1943, with a total of 671 Marder II vehicles being produced. As all Panzer II chassis were being switched to production of the Wespe SPG, production of the Marder II terminated prematurely. However, due to the success of the vehicle more were required, and so between July 1943 and March 1944 a further 73 were built. The fighting compartment was open-topped and open-backed but the

RIGHT: **A mid-production Marder III in Italy in 1944. This vehicle has the gun and fighting compartment in the middle of the vehicle, but a much larger armoured shield has been placed around this compartment. The compact size of the Marder can be clearly seen.**

LEFT: **The driver's position is forward and under the main gun, and has very limited vision. This vehicle has been hit in the engine and destroyed by fire.**
ABOVE: **The very open fighting compartment of this early Marder shows up well here. The basket on top of the engine deck was used to store personal kit and ammunition.**

front was closed by the gun-shield of the main armament. The Marder II was both very agile and very reliable, and proved to be a very useful combat vehicle. It would see service on all fronts and remained in active service until the end of the war.

The Marder III, based on the PzKpfw 38(t) tank chassis, was built in two versions. By late 1941, the 38(t) was considered both obsolete as a main battle tank and too slow for the reconnaissance role, so all production was changed to the SPG chassis. The first version was very much a makeshift temporary vehicle, using the captured Russian 76.2mm/3in gun. Production started in March 1942 with 24 units per month being built, moving up to 30 units per month by July 1942, with a total production of 344 vehicles. Most were sent to the Eastern Front, but 66 went to join the *Afrika Korps* in North Africa. The gun crew were very exposed in this vehicle and the Russian gun put considerable strain on the 38(t) tank chassis.

The Germans had realized that the first version of the Marder III was wasteful and unsatisfactory but now that the

initial pressing needs of the army had been dealt with, it could be redesigned and improved. The new vehicle was very different to the original with the successful PaK40 gun for its main armament. The driver's compartment in the front was improved with the engine moved to the middle of the vehicle behind the driver and the fighting compartment moved to the rear. These alterations made for a more balanced vehicle and gave the crew better protection, but it was still open-topped. It was built by BMM (*Böhmisch-Mährische Maschinenfabrik*). The original company designation had to be changed as it had a Jewish name in the title, but after the war the company reverted to its original name. Production stopped in May 1944 when the manufacturing facilities were switched to the Hetzer Tank Destroyer, by which time a total of 975 vehicles had been produced.

All the Marder vehicles performed well above their expected level and were a real problem to the Allied troops that came across them. They proved to be very reliable and by January 1945 some 300 were still in action in the German Army.

LEFT: **This is a late-production version of the Marder III. The gun position has been moved to the rear of the vehicle and the front has been completely redesigned. This Marder has a full load of ammunition in the gun position but has been damaged in an air raid.**

Marder III Self-Propelled Anti-Tank Gun

Country: Germany
Entered service: 1943
Crew: 4
Weight: 10,668kg/10.5 tons
Dimensions: Length – 4.95m/16ft 3in
　　Height – 2.5m/8ft 2in
　　Width – 2.15m/7ft 1in
Armament: Main – 7.5cm/2.95in PaK40/3 gun
　　Secondary – 7.92mm/0.312in MG34 machine-gun
Armour: Maximum – 15mm/0.59in
Powerplant: Praga EPA 6-cylinder 112kW/150hp petrol engine
Performance: Speed – 42kph/26mph
　　Range – 190km/120 miles

LEFT: **A crew member is standing in the roof-mounted reloading hatch next to the 10-round Nebelwerfer. The elevation and rotation of the unit was done from inside the vehicle.** BELOW: **A design picture for the mounting of the 8cm R-Vielfachwerfer. This fired 24 fin-stabilized rockets and was adopted by the Waffen SS.**

Maultier Nebelwerfer 15cm Panzerwerfer

The Maultier (Mule) was developed following the German experiences in Russia when ordinary wheeled vehicles became immobilized by mud and snow. The original Maultier half-track was built by the SS Division *Das Reich*, who fitted a Carden-Loyd track system to a Ford V8 truck. This proved so very successful that an order came down from high command to develop the idea further. Some 20,000 of these vehicles were built by three manufacturers.

In late 1942 Opel were asked to develop a spacious armoured body for the Maultier. Some 289 of these were to be used as ammunition carriers and 300 others were to be fitted with the Nebelwerfer 15cm/5.91in rocket launcher. The body of the vehicle was an all-welded construction and its simple design made mass production easy. The front wheels retained normal brakes operated by a foot pedal while the tracks were braked by two hand-operated leavers beside the driver. The engine was in the front of the vehicle with the driver's compartment behind. The driver and commander sat side by side with a third crew member behind them. The reload rocket storage was in the body of the vehicle, with a large hatch in the roof for the crew to reload the launch tubes in safety. When the Nebelwerfer fired it left great smoke trails behind pinpointing the battery position but by fitting the weapon to a half-track vehicle, the rockets could be fired then the vehicle could quickly move to a new position. The ten-barrelled Nebelwerfer 42 was subsequently developed with five tubes layered in two rows mounted on a 360-degree mount fitted to the rear of the vehicle. To fire all ten rockets took just 10 seconds and a reload was completed in 90 seconds. These vehicles were organized into companies with each company having eight vehicles carrying 80 launch tubes.

The Nebelwerfer was nicknamed "Moaning Minnie" by Allied troops, due to the noise the rocket made in flight. These Panzerwerfer units were deployed mainly on the Eastern Front and in France.

RIGHT: **Under the rocket tubes can be seen the small sighting window, which has two manual sliding shutters. The large rear doors give access into the ammunition storage area which is at the rear. This half-track is well equipped with storage lockers down each side of the vehicle.**

Maultier 15cm Panzerwerfer	

Country: Germany
Entered service: 1943
Crew: 3
Weight: 8,636kg/8.5 tons
Dimensions: Length – 6m/19ft 6in
  Height – 3.05m/10ft
  Width – 2.2m/7ft 3in
Armament: Main – 10 x 15cm/5.91in Nebelwerfer
  Secondary – 7.92mm/0.312in MG34 machine-gun
Armour: Maximum – 10mm/0.394in
Powerplant: Opel 3.6-litre 6-cylinder 51kW/68hp petrol engine
Performance: Speed – 40kph/25mph
  Range – 130km/81 miles

Minerva Armoured Car

The Belgians were the progenitors of armoured car warfare and would demonstrate to the world how flexible and useful the armoured car could be, yet in spite of this, Minerva armoured cars are not well known outside Belgium. Lieutenant Charles Henkart allowed two of his cars to be converted into armoured cars at the Cockerill Works in Hoboken and these cars were soon in action gathering intelligence and causing disruption among the German cavalry at the beginning of World War I.

The Minerva armoured car was based on the chassis of a 28kW/38hp touring car while the engine was a Knight-type four-cylinder double-sleeve valve which had proved itself in racing. The body of the car was covered in 4mm/0.16in armour plate, with the fighting compartment protected by two layers of armour spaced 3mm/0.12in apart. However, this armour was only just about bullet- and shell-splash-proof. The fighting compartment was in the middle of the vehicle and was open-topped, with a large single light fitted to the front next to the driver. The normal armament was a single Hotchkiss machine-gun on a pintle mount with an armoured shield, but some vehicles had a single 37mm/1.46in Puteaux cannon fitted. In 1918 the Belgians modified the Minerva by placing a basic open-backed turret over the machine-gun to give the gunner better protection.

The Belgians converted several more cars in 1914 and used them very much in the guerrilla role, harassing the German advanced troops. They also gave a lot of support to local troops during the withdrawal of forces in front of the

ABOVE LEFT: One of the early Minerva cars. The armoured doors in front of the radiator are half-open and the driver's visor is fully open. Extra storage boxes have been fitted to the car. ABOVE: The three-man crew of this car pose for a picture. The headlight has been moved on to the frontal plate of the vehicle next to the driver. The gun crew have very little protection when operating the gun.

German advance of 1914. By October 1914 the trench line had reached the coast and ended the mobile armoured car war. Like the British, the Belgians sent an armoured car section to help the Russians in their fight against the Germans, and these were shipped home in early 1918 and refurbished, following the Revolution and Russia's withdrawal from the war.

The Minerva armoured cars were to remain in service until the early 1930s. Some were even passed to the Gendarmerie and these would remain in police service until 1937.

ABOVE: A column of late-production Minerva cars. Some of the vehicles are carrying an extra crew member. The RNAS heard about these cars and very quickly copied the idea, and so the armoured car was born.

Minerva Armoured Car

Country: Belgium
Entered service: 1914
Crew: 3
Weight: 4,064kg/4 tons
Dimensions: Length – 4.9m/16ft 1in
   Height – 2.3m/7ft 6in
   Width – 1.75m/5ft 9in
Armament: Main – 8mm/0.315in Hotchkiss machine-gun
   Secondary – Small arms
Armour: Maximum – 11mm/0.43in
Powerplant: Minerva 4-cylinder sleeve valve 30kW/40hp petrol engine
Performance: Speed – 40kph/25mph
   Range – 240km/150 miles

Model 93 Sumida Armoured Car

The Sumida was designed by Japanese engineers to be able to run equally well on roads or railways, as it was intended to be used to police large areas. Development started in 1931; the vehicle went into production in 1933 and entered service in the same year.

It was a standard 6x4 chassis but with a few novel modifications to enable the car to carry out its dual role. The vehicle had one set of six wheels for road use and another for rails. These were easily interchangeable using four jacks built into the underside of the car, the spare set of six wheels being mounted in clips on the side of the fighting compartment. The driver and commander sat in the front of the vehicle with the other four crew members behind. There was a one-man turret mounted on the top of the fighting compartment with small arms firing slits in the sides. These vehicles were mainly operational in Manchuria, covering vast areas. These cars would always operate in pairs.

LEFT: **This Model 93 is being used as a railway patrol vehicle. It has its railway wheels fitted while its rubber road wheels are stored on the side of the vehicle. The radiator armoured doors are in the open position.**

Model 93 Sumida Armoured Car

Country: Japan
Entered service: 1933
Crew: 6
Weight: 7,620kg/7.5 tons
Dimensions: Length – 6.55m/21ft 6in
  Height – 2.97m/9ft 8in
  Width – 1.9m/6ft 3in
Armament: Main – 6.5mm/0.256in machine-gun
  Secondary – Small arms
Armour: Maximum – 16mm/0.63in
Powerplant: 6-cylinder 75kW/100hp petrol engine
Performance: Speed – 60kph/37mph
  Range – 240km/150 miles

Morris CS9/LAC Armoured Car Reconnaissance

Between 1935 and 1936 the Royal Ordnance Factory at Woolwich built two prototype armoured cars using the Morris 762kg/15cwt as the chassis, but both were turned down by the British Army. The third one was much better as the chassis was lengthened by 457mm/18in, engine power was increased and the turret design was changed. The new turret was open-topped and was now armed with a Boys anti-tank rifle and a Bren gun, while between the two guns was a smoke discharger. The Morris CS9 entered service with the British Army in 1938 with a total production run of only 100 vehicles.

The BEF took 38 of these vehicles to France in 1939 and all were lost in the withdrawal to the Channel Ports. In North Africa the CS9 would remain in service until 1941, but by fitting a radio it became a troop leader's car, while some of these vehicles were converted to command cars. However, the steering and suspension did not hold up well over rough terrain or in the deserts of North Africa.

LEFT: **This is a troop commander's vehicle in the deserts of North Africa in 1942. The crew have found some additional shade. The Boys AT rifle is fitted in the front of the turret while the Bren gun is fitted to the rear.**

Morris CS9/LAC Armoured Car Reconnaissance

Country: UK
Entered service: 1938
Crew: 4
Weight: 4,267kg/4.2 tons
Dimensions: Length – 4.78m/15ft 8in
  Height – 2.21m/7ft 3in
  Width – 2.06m/6ft 9in
Armament: Main – Boys 14mm/0.55in
  anti-tank rifle
  Secondary – 1 x Bren 7.7mm/0.303 machine-gun, and 1 x 51mm/2in smoke discharger
Armour: Maximum – 7mm/0.27in
Powerplant: Morris Commercial 4-cylinder 52kW/70hp petrol engine
Performance: Speed – 72kph/45mph
  Range – 386km/240 miles

LEFT AND BELOW: **This Morris armoured car seen here in Normandy has a cut-down turret, and the other gunner's hatches are in the open position. The car below has a full-size turret, but this afforded the gunner a very limited view, so in combat the crews cut the turret down as a field modification.**

Morris Mk 1 Light Reconnaissance Car

The Morris Mk 1 was one of the better British designs of a number of armoured cars produced during 1940 and 1941. Morris was subsequently given a contract to produce 1,000 of these Light Reconnaissance cars, with the first entering service in 1941.

The body of the car was a monocoque design of all-welded armour plate construction. The vehicle had a solid rear axle with independent suspension on the front wheels, but it was only two-wheel drive which would prove to be a problem in the cross-country role. The engine was mounted in the rear of the vehicle with the crew compartment in the front, while there were two large doors, one on each side, for the crew to enter and exit. The driver

sat in the middle of the crew compartment on the centreline of the vehicle with the turret gunner on the right side and the vehicle commander on the left. The vehicle commander would also operate the Boys anti-tank rifle, which could be fired to the front and rear only. The machine-gun turret had all-round traverse and a 51mm/2in smoke discharger mounted on its side.

Morris produced the Mk 2 version in 1942 and received an order for 1,050 of these new vehicles. The main improvements were that the vehicle was made into a 4x4 and the suspension was changed to leaf spring. The Boys anti-tank rifle was done away with and replaced with a second machine-gun. Large numbers of these armoured cars

were passed over to the RAF to be used as airfield defence vehicles. Some were also converted to turretless observation vehicles and a number of these would be taken to France by the RAF in 1944. When being used by the RAF as a Forward Observation Vehicle the gun turret was retained but the vehicle commander's position was converted to a radio position.

These armoured cars proved to be very serviceable and reliable and would remain in service in secondary roles until the end of the war.

LEFT: **The side door into the crew compartment is small, making access difficult. The crew compartment itself is compact with no space for the storage of personal kit. The turret on this vehicle has been fitted with a smoke discharger and is armed with a Bren gun.**

Morris Mk 1 Light Reconnaissance Car

Country: UK
Entered service: 1941
Crew: 3
Weight: 3,759kg/3.7 tons
Dimensions: Length – 4.06m/13ft 4in
   Height – 1.88m/6ft 2in
   Width – 2.03m/6ft 8in
Armament: Main – 14mm/0.55in Boys
   anti-tank rifle
   Secondary – Bren 7.7mm/0.303in machine-gun
Armour: Maximum – 14mm/0.55in
Powerplant: Morris 4-cylinder 53kW/71hp
   petrol engine
Performance: Speed – 72kph/45mph
   Range – 233km/145 miles

Ole Bill Bus

The name for this unusual AFV comes from a World War I cartoon character. The bus was a B-Type built by AEC for the London General Omnibus Company (LGOC) that had entered service on the streets of London in 1911. The LGOC allocated 300 B-Type buses to the British Army for use in France from October 1914 and they would remain on active service until 1918 when they helped bring the British Army home.

The first buses manned by volunteer crews arrived in France just in time to help move men forward during the First Battle of Ypres (October 19–November 22, 1914). They turned up painted in London red and cream livery with all the advertising still in place but were soon painted khaki and the windows were removed and boarded up. Wooden planking 51mm/2in thick was attached as armour but this was only effective against small shell splinters. Each bus could carry 25 fully armed men; the first unit carried being a London Scottish battalion. Some 900 buses would serve in France.

LEFT: **The first London buses sent out to France were required to enter service immediately so were seen moving behind the British lines in their full London livery.**

Ole Bill Bus B-Type

Country: UK
Entered service: 1914 Military service
Crew: 2
Weight: 4,064kg/4 tons
Dimensions: Length – 6.86m/22ft 6in
  Height – 3.79m/12ft 5in
  Width – 2.11m/6ft 11in
Armament: Main – None
  Secondary – None
Armour: Maximum – 51mm/2in wooden planking
Powerplant: AEC 4-cylinder 22kW/30hp petrol engine
Performance: Speed – 32km/20mph
  Range – 241km/150 miles

Otter Light Reconnaissance Car

The Otter, intended as a Canadian replacement for the British Humber Scout Car, was designed in early 1942 and went into production soon after. The vehicle turned out to be under-powered and had very poor visibility for the driver and crew, but despite these shortcomings, it was still placed into production. The vehicle had an all-welded construction with four-wheel drive and had a fair cross-country performance but, due to its height, a high centre of gravity. Total production of these vehicles was 1,761, with manufacturing finishing in 1943.

The Otter entered service with Canadian and British forces in late 1942, seeing action in Italy and northern Europe. The vehicle was very popular with its crews as it proved to be very reliable and was an easy vehicle to maintain in the field. The RAF regiment also used it as there was room in the body of the vehicle to carry extra radio equipment. The RAF increased the armament on its Otters including, among other weapons, an anti-aircraft machine-gun.

LEFT: **The Boys AT rifle has its own port in the front of the vehicle, while above this is a smoke discharger. This vehicle is covered in personal kit as there is no space for it inside the car.**

Otter Light Reconnaissance Car

Country: Canada
Entered service: 1942
Crew: 3
Weight: 4,877kg/4.8 tons
Dimensions: Length – 4.5m/14ft 9in
  Height – 2.44m/8ft
  Width – 2.13m/7ft
Armament: Main – 14mm/0.55in Boys anti-tank rifle
  Secondary – 1 x Bren 7.7mm/0.303in light machine-gun, and 1 x 101.6mm/4in smoke discharger
Armour: Maximum – 12mm/0.47in
Powerplant: GMC 6-cylinder 79kW/106hp petrol engine
Performance: Speed – 72kph/45mph
  Range – 402km/250 miles

FAR LEFT: **This car is in post-World War II service with the French Army. The driver's side hatch is in the open position. The coaxial machine-gun is not fitted to the turret of this car.** LEFT: **This side view of the Panhard, in French camouflage colours, shows the main entrance and exit door in the side of the vehicle below the turret. The design of this car would influence many designs in the 1950s.** TOP: **A French Panhard in German service in Russia, 1943. The extensive use of rivets in the construction of the vehicle can be clearly seen. The rear of the crew compartment below the turret can be raised to improve ventilation and give better vision.**

Panhard AMD Type 178 Armoured Car

The AMD (*Automitrailleuse de Découverte*) was conceived as a replacement for some of the ageing French armoured cars of World War I. The prototype appeared in 1933 but development was very slow as money was in short supply. It entered service with the French Army in 1935 and was issued to both infantry and cavalry units. The AMD 178 was a very good clean design, with the interior divided into fighting/driving and engine compartments. The armour was sloped and the construction was all riveted. The car was a 4x4 vehicle and had good cross-country performance due to the engine being mounted in the rear.

Only 360 were in service when the Germans invaded France in 1940 but the French had distributed these vehicles among so many units in "penny packets" that the Germans were able to capture over 200 of the AMD 178s intact and, as it performed well, they were taken into German service. However,

the French managed to rescue 46 of these cars and had them repaired after which they were then sent to the new unoccupied Vichy territory and hidden from the Germans.

The Germans replaced the 25mm/ 0.98in gun with their 37mm/1.46in anti-tank gun. Some were also modified to run on railway track by replacing the road wheels with railway wheels. A number of these cars were also converted into command radio cars by fitting a large frame aerial over the top of the vehicle. Many of these converted vehicles as well as standard AMD 178s were sent to the Eastern Front to support the anti-partisan war that was taking place behind the German lines. When the Germans overran Vichy they captured the remaining 46 AMD 178 cars that were in French hands. These were converted into a wheeled tank by installing a larger turret on the vehicle and arming it with a 50mm/1.97in gun. Most of these remained in France.

The AMD 178 was the most advanced medium armoured car in French service in 1940, and was soon back in production when the Renault factory was restored to French control in August 1944. It would remain in French service for many years after World War II.

Panhard AMD Type 178 Armoured Car

Country: France
Entered service: 1935
Crew: 3
Weight: 8,636kg/8.5 tons
Dimensions: Length – 4.79m/15ft 8in
 Height – 2.31m/7ft 7in
 Width – 2.01m/6ft 7in
Armament: Main – 1 x 25mm/0.98in gun, and
 1 x 7.5mm/0.295in MG31 coaxial machine-gun
 Secondary – None
Armour: Maximum – 26mm/1.02in
Powerplant: Panhard SK 6.33-litre 4-cylinder
 78kW/105hp petrol engine
Performance: Speed – 72kph/45mph
 Range – 300km/186 miles

LEFT: **An improved version of the Flakpanzer called the "Wirbelwind". This vehicle mounted the 2cm/0.79in Flakvierling 38 in an armoured rotating turret, and provided good crew protection. The slow rotational speed of this new turret was the one drawback of the design.** BELOW: **The first Flakpanzer to be issued to the Panzer formations was called the "Möbelwagen" (Furniture Van). To operate the gun you had to drop the sides of the vehicle.**

Panzer IV Flakpanzer

The problem of supplying the German Army with mobile anti-aircraft guns for protection from fighter bombers first came to light during the campaign in North Africa in 1942, when the RAF Desert Air Force destroyed large numbers of vehicles. To give the army convoys basic protection a number of very ad hoc conversions were made to allow some vehicles to carry a single 2cm/0.79in flak gun. However, this problem was passed back to the German High Command for a permanent solution to be found.

The first vehicle to based on the Panzer IV chassis was the Möbelwagen (Furniture Van) which was shown to Hitler on May 14, 1943, but he rejected it on the grounds that it was too expensive and that fighter bombers were not currently a great problem. The Möbelwagen was a basic Panzer IV chassis with

ABOVE: **The Flakpanzer Wirbelwind was seen as a stop-gap solution, allowing a quick conversion of the Panzer IV chassis. With this vehicle the driver could remain at his position for a fast response.**

the flak gun mounted in a box structure fixed to the top of the vehicle. When the gun went into action, the sides of the box were lowered exposing the gun and crew. The gun was the quadruple 2cm/0.79in Flakvierling 38, which had a high rate of fire but was magazine-fed. The vehicle was again shown to Hitler in October 1943 and was yet again rejected, this time due to its overall height being over 3m/9ft 10in and reservations that the crew had very little protection.

As the situation deteriorated on the Eastern Front and in Italy, an interim order was placed for the Möbelwagen, now armed with the 3.7cm/1.46in Flak 43. From February 1944, 20 of these vehicles were produced per month. The vehicle had a crew of seven, though in service this was often reduced to five, and could carry 416 rounds which gave three minutes firing time for the Flak 43. The first of these vehicles entered service in April 1944 and total production by the end of the war was 240 Möbelwagens.

The first true Flakpanzer was the Wirbelwind, which had been shown to General Guderian in May 1944. He requested that it be put into production straight away. These vehicles were built using old Panzer IV chassis returned from the front, with a total of 105 conversions being completed. There was a

LEFT: The "Ostwind" version of the Flakpanzer IV which mounted a single 3.7cm/1.46in Flak 36. This vehicle could also be used against ground targets.
ABOVE: Inside the driver's position of a Flakpanzer IV. The driver's vision block is top centre, the track control arms are in the middle, with the gear lever and other controls to the right of the seat.

crew of five; four were in the turret manning the gun, while the driver remained at his post. The turret was made from angled 16mm/0.63in armour plates welded into position, the angle of the plates helping to close the open top a little. The vehicle was armed with the quadruple 2cm/0.79in Flakvierling 38, which was enclosed in the armoured, but still open-topped, turret. The Wirbelwind entered production in July 1944, but the gun was not delivering the results required and so production stopped in November 1944.

The Ostwind was to replace the Wirbelwind, still using the Panzer IV chassis but with a new gun fitted. The new gun was the 3.7cm/1.46in Flak 43 as used on the Möbelwagen which was fitted into the same turret as had been used on the Wirbelwind. The Ostwind II had the same body and turret as the Ostwind, but with the armament changed to a twin 3cm/1.18in Flakzwilling 44 guns, with the twin barrels mounted side by side. This vehicle only reached the prototype stage before the war ended.

On April 20, 1944 Hitler ordered that the twin 3cm/1.18in Doppelflak 303 that was just going into production for the U-Boat service should be fitted to a Panzer IV chassis. This new vehicle would be called the Kugelblitz Anti-Aircraft Tank and would replace all the other flak vehicles in production. By February 1945 when production stopped only two full vehicles and five chassis had been built. Other chassis were also being considered for the new flak tanks and these included the PzKpfw 38(t) and the Panther.

In 1944 Flakpanzer Platoons were formed and were assigned to Panzer regiments. These were normally formed of 8 Möbelwagen or 4 Möbelwagen and 4 Wirbelwind per platoon. The vast majority of these Flak vehicles were sent to France in an attempt to protect the German tanks from the virtually unchallenged Allied air force. Most of these vehicles were either destroyed or captured in the Falaise Pocket in Normandy. The rest were abandoned during the retreat across the Seine.

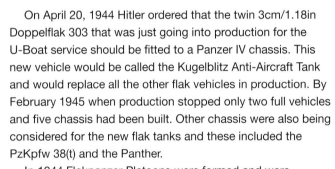

LEFT: The Möbelwagen in the firing position. When the sides are dropped, the driver has very poor vision. When operating the weapon, the gun crew are very exposed. They have to travel in the open-topped box with the gun. This vehicle has a number of spare track links attached to the front of the hull to increase the armour.

Möbelwagen

Country: Germany
Entered service: 1944
Crew: 5
Weight: 24,384kg/24 tons
Dimensions: Length – 5.92m/19ft 5in
　　　　　Height – 2.73m/8ft 11in
　　　　　Width – 2.95m/9ft 8in
Armament: Main – 3.7cm/1.46in Flak 43
　　　　　Secondary – 7.92mm/0.312in MG34
　　　　　machine-gun
Armour: Maximum – 50mm/1.97in
Powerplant: Maybach HL 120 TRM 112
　　　　　203kW/272hp 12-cylinder petrol engine
Performance: Speed – 38kph/24mph
　　　　　Range – 200km/124 miles

LEFT: **This Priest of the 1st Armoured Division in North Africa is being readied for action. The lack of storage provision can be clearly seen as the vehicle is covered with personal kit, camouflage netting and bedding.** BELOW: **An American M7 on trial in America. When these vehicles went overseas, the large white star was made smaller. The crews very quickly found that the star was an aiming point for the Germans, so either painted it out or covered it in mud.**

Priest 105mm Self-Propelled Gun

Reports coming out of North Africa in 1940 had shown the Americans the urgent need for an SPG and as an interim solution the T19 half-track was introduced into service. In early 1941, an alternative solution of mounting the 105mm/4.13in howitzer on the M3 tank chassis was proposed. The weapon was mounted in an open fighting compartment and was offset to the right to give room for the driver. Trials of the vehicle proved to be very successful and reliable, and the British Tank Mission in America placed orders immediately it was shown to them. Known to the US Forces as the M7, the British named it the "Priest" as the AA machine-gun was mounted in what looked like a pulpit and all Royal Artillery SPGs were given ecclesiastical names.

American Loco started production in April 1942 and by the end of the year had produced 2,028 vehicles of a total M7 production of 3,490 vehicles. The first British order was for

2,500 in the first year and 3,000 by the end of 1943, but this was never met as the American forces were armed with the new weapon first. The Priest had identical chassis and automotive parts as the M3 tank but, just as the M4 Sherman tank was replacing the M3 Grant in service, so from late 1943 the M4 chassis replaced the M3 chassis in Priest production. In American service, this new vehicle using M4 chassis and automotive parts was known as the M7B1. The height of the fighting compartment sides was raised by the fitting of hinged plates to give the ammunition better protection as there was storage for 69 rounds in open bins. Nine hundred and fifty-three of these vehicles were built from March 1944 to March 1945.

LEFT: **This British Priest is being unloaded from an LCT (Landing Craft Tank). The driver's visor is in the open position but because of the poor vision, the "pulpit" gunner is helping direct the vehicle off the craft.**

LEFT: **The driver has good forward vision on his side of the main gun, but can see nothing on the machine-gunner's side of the vehicle. Here you can see the high driving position in the vehicle which has the effect of making the vehicle tall.** ABOVE: **The storage boxes on the front of the vehicle are for spare track links. The running gear and chassis for these vehicles came from the M4 Sherman. The machine-gun position has a circular swivel mount on the top of it.**

In September 1942, 90 Priest SPGs were sent to the British 8th Army in North Africa and took part in the second Battle of El Alamein. From this time onwards it became the standard issue to British medium SP batteries. The British units equipped with the Priest that landed in Normandy during June 1944 soon had their vehicles replaced by the Sexton SPG, but the Priest remained in service with the 8th Army for the remainder of the war as it fought all the way up Italy. One problem encountered there was that the howitzer could not be elevated enough to reach targets high up in the mountains, so the vehicle would be driven up on to a log ramp to increase the angle of elevation. This same problem would arise again during the Korean War and at first was solved in the same way as in Italy until a modification was made raising the gun by 155mm/6in, so creating the M7B2.

The Canadians, like the British, stopped using their M7 Priests soon after D-Day as they were replaced by the new 25pdr Sexton. However, General Simonds, commander of the Canadian II Corps, got permission to keep the M7 chassis for troop-carrying purposes, so at the end of July these chassis were sent to the Canadian field workshop codenamed "Kangaroo" for conversion. The main armament and all its internal fittings were removed and the aperture for the gun was plated over, but the "pulpit" with its machine-gun was kept to give covering fire to the troops as they debussed, and the side plates were raised to give the men more protection. These vehicles could carry 20 fully armed infantry and had a crew of two; they were a great success and would lead to a whole new type of infantry vehicle. The Canadians used a number of these "Unfrocked Priests" to drive their infantry through the German lines during Operation "Totalize". By August 6, 1944, 75 "Priest Kangaroos", as they were later named, were ready and the infantry had just one day to learn how to use them, the drivers for the new vehicle being taken from the artillery units that had used the Priest. This conversion proved very popular and more Priests were converted into Kangaroos in Italy. In addition, a number of redundant Priests were converted to artillery observation vehicles by removing the gun and putting extra radios, telephones and map tables into the resulting space.

LEFT: **A battery of Priest SPGs camouflaged up in Normandy on June 6, 1944. The sides of the vehicle have been increased in height by the fitting of the deep-water wading gear. The front of the vehicle is covered in spares for the running gear.**

Priest 105mm SPG

Country: USA
Entered service: 1942
Crew: 7
Weight: 26,010kg/25.6 tons
Dimensions: Length – 6.02m/19ft 9in
    Height – 2.54m/8ft 4in
    Width – 2.88m/9ft 5in
Armament: Main – 105mm/4.13in M1A2 howitzer
    Secondary – 12.7mm/0.5in machine-gun
Armour: Maximum – 62mm/2.44in
Powerplant: Continental 9-cylinder radial
    280kW/375hp petrol engine
Performance: Speed – 41.8kph/26mph
    Range – 201km/125 miles

Renault and Peugeot Armoured Cars

The French formed their armoured car units in 1914. At first these used touring cars but they were soon replaced by rudimentary armoured cars such as the Renault and Peugeot. At the start of World War I, Renault was the largest car construction company in France. By November 1914 they had produced 100 AM Renault 20CV mod.E1 armoured cars which entered service in December 1914 crewed by French marines. At first the armour was poor but this was very quickly upgraded to 5mm/0.2in, while the famous Renault engine cover was retained and armoured. The vehicle was open-topped with an 8mm/0.315in Hotchkiss machine-gun mounted on a pintle mount. A heavier 37mm/1.46in Puteaux gun was carried by some Renault cars and these would be used in many actions as close-support vehicles especially during the retreat and advances of 1918.

The Peugeot 18CV was the other main French armoured car in 1914. They were designed by Captain Reynauld who made both the machine-gun car and the heavy gun car the same so armament could be interchangeable in these open-topped vehicles. The first ones were armed with an 8mm/0.315in machine-

gun, but this was soon supplemented by fitting a 37mm/1.46in gun to some of the cars. These vehicles were built on the Peugeot 146 chassis at first and later the 148 chassis was used, giving a total production run of 150 of these armoured cars. The Peugeot cars initially saw active service in January 1915 when the first cars were sent to join the 7th Cavalry Division and formed the 6th and 7th Armoured Car Groups. There was a crew of three on the machine-gun car and four on the 37mm/1.46in heavy gun car. They could also carry five infantry if required and during the great German retreat of

1918 they were used to great effect in harassing the German infantry. By the end of World War I, the French had only 28 Peugeot armoured cars still fit for service. Poland bought 18 of these in 1918 and some were still in Polish service when the Germans invaded in 1939.

ABOVE: **This Renault armoured car has a crew of four and is armed with a single 37mm/1.46in gun, which has an armoured shield around it. This car has its starting handle in place in the front of the vehicle between the wheels.** LEFT: **Five Peugeot machine-gun armed armoured cars at Magnicourt in May 1915. The third car in is armed with a 47mm/1.85in gun. The large single door is mounted in the side of the vehicle behind the driver and in front of the gun.**

Peugeot 18CV Armoured Car

Country: France
Entered service: 1915
Crew: 3 plus 5 infantry
Weight: 5,000kg/4.9 tons
Dimensions: Length – 4.8m/16ft
  Height – 2.8m/9ft 2in
  Width – 1.8m/5ft 11in
Armament: Main – 8mm/0.315in Hotchkiss
  Mle 14 machine-gun
  Secondary – Small arms
Armour: Maximum – 5mm/0.2in
Powerplant: Peugeot 146 4-cylinder 34kW/45hp
  petrol engine
Performance: Speed – 40kph/25mph
  Range – 140km/87 miles

LEFT: **The driver is in his position and all his hatches are open. The hatch is split in two parts with the dome part folding backwards. The other crew position is all "buttoned up".** BELOW: **This UE is pulling a small four-wheel trailer, which has been fitted with cross-country tracks. Behind this is the Hotchkiss 25mm/0.98in AT gun.**

Renault UE Infantry Tractor

Production of these light tractors had started in 1931 at Renault and in 1936 at AMX, and by 1940 the French had some 6,000 in service. These vehicles were not designed for combat but to act as an armoured supply vehicle, the hardship of Verdun having shown the necessity for such a design. Some of these vehicles were produced with a machine-gun for the co-driver but these were far and few between.

Renault based these vehicles on the Carden-Loyd Mk VI carrier design. It was of a riveted construction, with a Renault engine. The crew were fully protected as they sat in the main body of the vehicle with the engine between them and only had their heads protruding. These were protected by armoured domes that were

hinged in the middle so that the front part could lift like a knight's visor. Behind the crew was a storage box for supplies but it was very small and could not carry more than 150kg/331lb. The vehicle was always designed to pull an armoured trailer, which was open-topped. These four-wheeled trailers were capable of carrying 500kg/1,102lb and for extreme conditions could be fitted with caterpillar tracks to improve their overall cross-country performance.

The Germans captured so many of these vehicles that they would see service in many areas and in many forms. A large number were converted into light Panzerjager, armed at first with a 37mm/1.46in PaK35/36, and many of these were used by garrison forces in

France. When Rommel took over the coastal defences in France, he instructed that a lot of the Renault UEs should be converted into rocket carriers. They were fitted with four Wurfrahmen 40 rockets mounted in either of two ways on the vehicle. One method was to put side-skirts on the vehicle with two rockets placed on each side, while the other means was a box structure built over the rear supply box and again capable of carrying and firing four rockets. These were first encounter by the Allies in Normandy, but later more widely throughout the European theatre.

LEFT: **This UE is being inspected by a group of British soldiers in France in 1944. The short exhaust can be seen. This was the cause of a few problems with fumes going into the crew compartments.**

Renault UE Infantry Tractor

Country: France
Entered service: 1931
Crew: 2
Weight: 2,032kg/2 tons
Dimensions: Length – 2.69m/8ft 10in
　　Height – 1.03m/3ft 5in
　　Width – 1.7m/5ft 7in
Armament: Main – None
　　Secondary – Small arms
Armour: Maximum – 7mm/0.27in
Powerplant: Renault 4-cylinder 63kW/85hp petrol engine
Performance: Speed – 30kph/19mph
　　Range – 180km/112 miles

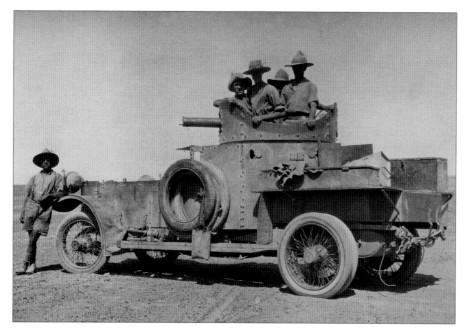

LEFT: Dominion troops in Palestine during World War I. The car has an open-topped turret allowing for much-needed additional ventilation in the hot climate. The desert was very hard on tyres, hence all the spares carried on the side of the car.
ABOVE: A column of Rolls-Royce cars stopped in a village behind the Western Front. The rear wheels have been fitted with chains to improve traction in the mud. The cars are covered in personal kit.

Rolls-Royce Armoured Car

When the Royal Naval Air Service (RNAS) was sent to France in 1914, it went with a very mixed array of aircraft and vehicles. After observing the Belgian Army using their armoured cars and how they were harassing the advancing German forces, the RNAS decided to join in, sending two Rolls-Royce Silver Ghost cars to a depot in Dunkirk for conversion into armoured cars. These were covered in boiler plate and armed with a machine-gun. This proved to be so successful that the Royal Navy agreed to develop the design into a proper armoured car using the Rolls-Royce Silver Ghost tourer as the chassis.

The chassis had its suspension strengthened and was fitted with 9mm/0.354in armour and a new large single turret. This turret was referred to as the "Admiralty Pattern" and would be fitted to all but the last model. It was shaped like a bishop's mitre and was fitted with a single heavy machine-gun, either a Vickers or a Maxim belt-fed 7.7mm/0.303in. In very hot weather the top could be removed to give better ventilation. The radiator had armoured doors and a large open space

was left behind the turret for the carriage of stores or another machine-gun. The first of these new cars arrived in France in late 1914 and were issued to the RNAS.

Once the "Race for the Sea" had reached the North Sea coast and the Western Front trench line was established, there was very little for the RNAS armoured cars to do. In 1915 the Navy handed over most of their cars to the British Army, which did not really want them initially as it had no idea how to use them. Some officers, like the Duke of Westminster and Colonel Lawrence (Lawrence of Arabia), took to these new weapons and, using them with dash and flair in the deserts of the Middle East, demonstrated to the army how to get the best from these machines. Seeing the potential but faced with several types of armoured car, the army decided to standardize on the Rolls-Royce and formed them into Light Armoured Motor (LAM) batteries of the Motor Machine-gun Corps. The Rolls-Royce armoured car was then sent to several other fronts during World War I, such as the North West Frontier in India, German South West Africa and Persia (later Iran). These 1914 Pattern

LEFT: A Rolls-Royce car bogged down in the mud of the Western Front. The car has been camouflaged in typical British World War I scheme. Note that the machine-gun has been removed. RIGHT: A Rolls-Royce 1924 Pattern Mk 1, with a modified turret, patrolling the border in Egypt in 1940.

LEFT: **This was originally a 1924 Pattern Rolls-Royce armoured car. By 1940 the chassis of these cars were worn out, so in August 1940 a number of Rolls-Royce cars were fitted with a Fordson chassis in Cairo, Egypt. These cars were armed with a Boys AT rifle, a Vickers machine-gun in the turret and a pair of Vickers K guns on the top of the turret.**

cars would remain in service officially until replaced by the Rolls-Royce 1920 Pattern.

This new car was placed into production after World War I and a number of the 1914 type were modernized to the 1920 Pattern. The wire-spoked wheels became disc-type, while the turret sides were made higher and louver doors were fitted to the radiator. The Air Ministry also produced these new 1920 Pattern cars for the RAF, but with wider tyres as they were operating in the deserts of Persia and Iraq. They would see service in many parts of the British Empire, being used to "police the Empire".

In 1924 a new pattern car went into production with a number of small changes and improvements. The body of the car was altered: a cupola for the vehicle commander was fitted to the turret and a new gun mounting was fitted to help close a weakness. A number of the 1920 cars were brought up to this

new pattern. Others were sold to various countries around the world and would see service in World War II.

There were a few problems with the Rolls-Royce, one being that there was a small fuel tank fitted in the dashboard and another that brakes were only fitted to the rear wheels, so stopping was a problem at times. These cars were still in active service with the British Army when war was declared in 1939 and in some parts of the Empire there were even a few 1914 Pattern cars in military use. In all, there was a total of 83 Rolls-Royce armoured cars remaining, most of them in Egypt. These were fitted with a new open-topped turret carrying a Boys anti-tank rifle instead of the machine-gun. A twin Lewis gun was mounted on a pintle mount on the back of the vehicle in an anti-aircraft role. These vehicles would, however, only remain in service for a few more years.

LEFT: **A Rolls-Royce Admiralty Pattern turreted car at a Forward Aid Station in France in 1915. The front of this car has been fitted with a pivoted hook to pull away barbed wire entanglements.**

Rolls-Royce 1920 Pattern Armoured Car

Country: UK
Entered service: 1920
Crew: 3
Weight: 3,861kg/3.8 tons
Dimensions: Length – 5.18m/17ft
    Height – 2.33m/7ft 5in
    Width – 1.9m/6ft 3in
Armament: Main – 7.7mm/0.303in Vickers
    machine-gun
    Secondary – Small arms
Armour: Maximum – 9mm/0.354in
Powerplant: Rolls-Royce 6-cylinder 60kW/80hp
    petrol engine
Performance: Speed – 80kph/50mph
    Range – 240km/150 miles

Sd Kfz 7/1 8-ton Half-Track

The design of these vehicles goes back to 1926 and was personally championed by Ernst Kniepkamp, head of the *Heereswaffenamt*. During 1932, it was decided to standardize the half-tracks into light (5,080kg/5-ton), medium (8,128kg/8-ton), and heavy (12,193kg/12-ton), while in 1934 two more half-tracks, a 1,016kg/1-ton and a 3,048kg/3-ton, were added to the list. The last one to be developed was the giant 18,289kg/18-ton half-track in 1936. The first of these vehicles to go into production and enter service with the German Army was the Sd Kfz 7 8-ton half-track. The army used the *Zugkraftwagen* (Towing Tractor) as their main artillery towing vehicle, but this half-track went on to be used for many other purposes for which it was never originally designed during World War II.

Development and design of the Sd Kfz 7 was undertaken by Krauss-Maffei (KM) based in Munich-Allach. They would be the largest single producer, building 6,129 of these vehicles with the remaining 5,880 being built by various other manufacturers. Production continued to the end of World War II. The vehicle had an 8-ton trailer-towing capacity, and the suspension was leaf-spring on the early models but by 1940 this had been changed to torsion bar which was much more satisfactory. The engine would not change from the original Maybach throughout the entire production run, but the horsepower it developed would increase from

89kW/120hp to 119kW/160hp. The tracks were made up of metal plates with rubber inserts, which had sealed lubricated needle-roller bearings in them. This helped to give the vehicle long track life and ensured low rolling resistance.

Some of the KM production run were converted into supply vehicles by removing the rear crew area and replacing this with a wooden flat bed. Another significant conversion of 442 units into Flakvierling vehicles started in late 1943. In this case the driver's bench seat was retained with a second one placed back to back and an anti-aircraft gun, either the quadruple 2cm/0.79in Flak 38 or the 3.7cm/1.46in Flak 36, mounted on the flat-bed. As the fighter bomber threat increased, armoured cabs were fitted to the vehicle to give the crew better protection while travelling, though not for the gun crew while the vehicle was in action.

TOP: **The first of the Flak half-tracks was the 1,016kg/1-ton Sd Kfz 10 which entered service in 1938. The single gun required a crew of seven men.** ABOVE: **The Sd Kfz 10 in action against a ground target. The exposed crew position can be clearly seen.**

LEFT: **The Sd Kfz 7 Flak half-track in action in Russia. These vehicles still had a very exposed crew position but with the introduction of the Flakvierling 38 the firepower was quadrupled. These half-tracks proved to be deadly against both aircraft and ground targets.**

Sd Kfz 7/1 8-ton Half-Track

Country: Germany
Entered service: 1943
Crew: 10
Weight: 11,786kg/11.6 tons
Dimensions: Length – 6.85m/22ft 6in
Height – 2.62m/8ft 7in
Width – 2.4m/7ft 10in
Armament: Main – 4 x 2cm/0.79in Flak 38
Secondary – Small arms
Armour: Maximum – 8mm/0.315in
Powerplant: Maybach HL 62 6-cylinder TUK
104kW/140hp petrol engine
Performance: Speed – 50kph/31mph
Range – 250km/155 miles

Sd Kfz 8 and 9 Heavy Half-Tracks

These were two of the largest half-tracks produced by the Germans. In 1931, development was started by Daimler-Benz on the Sd Kfz 8, a 12,193kg/12-ton half-track. It was designed to be a heavy tractor for heavy artillery such as the 21cm/8.25in and the 10.5cm/4.13in Flak gun. The first 12-ton tractors were built by Krupp and Skoda from 1932 and between them they produced 315 of these vehicles. Daimler took over production from 1934, initially using the DB 7 chassis, and these vehicles would remain in production until late 1944 with the final mark of chassis used being the DB 11. In total, 3,973 of these half-tracks were built. In 1939, Krupp converted ten of these 12-ton half-tracks into self-propelled gun mounts by placing the 8.8cm/3.46in Flak 18 on the flat bed of the vehicle. The normal cab was done away with

and replaced with an armoured cupola for the driver, with ammunition stacked on the rear of the vehicle and the eight-man crew sitting unprotected under the gun. These weapons were built to destroy fortifications, as the gun had restricted movement and tended to destabilize the vehicle when fired.

The Sd Kfz 9 was an 18,289kg/18-ton heavy half-track; it was designed as a heavy tank recovery vehicle and as a prime mover for 24,385kg/24-ton recovery trailers. Four different models were built during the production run of 2,334 vehicles which would finish in late 1944. These vehicles were also used by the German engineers working for the bridging section. In 1940, 15 of these 18-ton half-tracks were converted into heavy self-propelled gun mounts for the 8.8cm/3.46in Flak 18. These guns were more manoeuvrable and stable on this

ABOVE: **The Sd Kfz 9 was the largest of the half-tracks produced by the Germans. These vehicles proved to be very good and stable firing platforms. The crew cab has been armoured, but when the crew operate the gun they have no protection. The wire-mesh sides of the vehicle have to be folded down before the gun can go into action.**

platform than on the Sd Kfz 8 and could be used for many tasks including anti-aircraft work. However, the main task of this vehicle, like the earlier 12-ton half-track version, was to destroy fortified positions. The engine and driver's position were covered in armour, with ammunition carried in a locker on the rear deck. There were also side-screens that were lowered when the gun was in action, increasing the rear deck area.

LEFT: **This version of the Sd Kfz 8 half-track was produced in 1939 and was designed to be a fortress-buster and heavy AT gun. The vehicles were very tall and the gun crew were very exposed on the rear of the vehicle.**

Sd Kfz 9 8.8cm SPG Half-Track

Country: Germany
Entered service: 1940
Crew: 9
Weight: 25,400kg/25 tons
Dimensions: Length – 9.32m/30ft 7in
    Height – 3.67m/12ft
    Width – 2.65m/8ft 8in
Armament: Main – 8.8cm/3.46in Flak 18
    Secondary – Small arms
Armour: Maximum – 14.5mm/0.57in
Powerplant: Maybach HL 108 TUKRM
    186kW/250hp 12-cylinder petrol engine
Performance: Speed – 50kph/31mph
    Range – 260km/162 miles

Sd Kfz 222 Armoured Car

The Germans started developing a new armoured car in 1934 with several criteria in mind: that the vehicle was reliable, that it could run off various grades of fuel, that it was a simple construction and that it had a good cross-country ability. The first of these new cars was the Sd Kfz 221, but this proved to be too small and lightly armed, so in 1937 development started on the Sd Kfz 222. Two standard chassis for four-wheeled armoured cars had been developed during 1936–7, the first of which had the engine mounted in the rear while the second had the engine mounted in the front. The latter type was used in the Sd Kfz 222.

The Sd Kfz 222 would become the standard light armoured car of the German Army until the end of World War II. This car entered service in 1938 and had heavier armament and a larger turret than the Sd Kfz 221. However, the new turret was still very small and cramped. It was open-topped but included a wire mesh screen that could be pulled over to protect the crew. This screen was divided in the middle and would hang over each side of the turret when open. When the screen was in the closed position, use of the main armament was even more difficult. The Sd Kfz 222 mounted one 2cm/0.79in cannon and a coaxial machine-gun, both of which could be elevated to 87 degrees so that the car could engage enemy aircraft. The cannon was mounted on a pintle which incorporated the elevation and traverse mechanism and had a firing button on the floor. At the rear of the vehicle the engine deck was sharply sloped to improve the driver's vision when reversing.

The Sd Kfz 222 suffered from a number of problems, particularly the poor cross-country performance and short range of the vehicle, which would lead to the car being removed from front-line service during the invasion of the Soviet Union in 1941. Production stopped in 1943 after 989 vehicles had been built.

TOP: **This Sd Kfz 222 armoured car has been caught in the open during an air attack. The turret has been removed from this vehicle and a larger wire mesh has been fitted.** ABOVE: **A mixed group of German armoured cars on exercise in 1938. The Sd Kfz 222 is on the right and has the turret-mounted screens in the raised position.**

Sd Kfz 222 Light Armoured Car

Country: Germany
Entered service: 1938
Crew: 3
Weight: 4,877kg/4.8 tons
Dimensions: Length – 4.8m/14ft 9in
  Height – 2m/6ft 7in
  Width – 1.95m/6ft 5in
Armament: Main – 2cm/0.79in KwK38
  Secondary – 7.92mm/0.312in MG34 machine-gun
Armour: Maximum – 30mm/1.18in
Powerplant: Horch/Auto Union 108 8-cylinder 60kW/81hp petrol engine
Performance: Speed – 80kph/50mph
  Range – 300km/187 miles

RIGHT: **This is the Sd Kfz 223 long-range radio car. This car uses the chassis, engine and the body of the Sd Kfz 222. The frame aerial folds back towards the rear of the vehicle and this aerial is in the down position.**

LEFT: **A standard Sd Kfz 231 coming down a slope. The long bonnet of the vehicle, which caused a number of problems for the driver, can clearly be seen. This car has the secondary hull machine-gun fitted.** ABOVE: **A heavy 6 Rad (six-wheeled) radio car. The frame aerial is fixed to the body of the vehicle at the rear and to two fixed uprights on the turret. The turret supports were quickly changed to a form that allowed the turret to rotate.**

Sd Kfz 231 Heavy Armoured Car 6 Rad

This German heavy armoured car was developed at the Kazan test centre in the Soviet Union in the 1920s. The first heavy car chassis to be developed were 8x8 and 10x10 but these were too expensive to be put into production. As a result the Germans decided to select a truck chassis already in production and fit an armoured body. The chassis selected was the Daimler-Benz 6x4, but other manufacturers' chassis were also used in production.

The Sd Kfz 231 had a front-mounted engine and the chassis was strengthened to take the extra weight of the armour. A second driving position was constructed in the rear of the fighting compartment so the vehicle could be driven in reverse. During trials it was discovered that the front axle needed strengthening and the radiators needed

to be improved. With these improvements, the car entered service with the German Army in 1932 and remained in production until 1935. Initially the armament was a single machine-gun in the turret, but this was quickly upgraded to a 2cm/0.79in KwK30 and coaxial MG34 machine-gun while there was provision for an anti-aircraft machine-gun on the roof of the turret. These vehicles did not perform particularly well as they were too heavy for the chassis, were underpowered, and had very poor cross-country ability. However, the car did provide the German Army with a very good training vehicle, as on hard roads the vehicle was as good as any of its contemporaries.

These armoured cars were used during the occupation of Austria in 1938 and of Czechoslovakia in 1939. They

would see combat during the invasion of Poland, and were used during the Blitzkrieg operations (the invasion of the Low Countries and France) in 1940. This vehicle looked very impressive in action and was used extensively in propaganda, receiving a lot of media coverage.

The Sd Kfz 232 was a long-range radio vehicle variant of the Sd Kfz 231. A basic Sd Kfz 231 was fitted with a large frame aerial fixed to the top of the vehicle and extra radio sets were installed in the fighting compartment.

LEFT: **Behind the front wheel is an engine grill and beside that is a small hull hatch which gives access to the hull gunner's position. The spare wheel is carried on the rear of the car.**

Sd Kfz 231 Heavy Armoured Car 6 Rad

Country: Germany
Entered service: 1932
Crew: 4
Weight: 5,791kg/5.7 tons
Dimensions: Length – 5.61m/18ft 4in
　　　Height – 2.24m/7ft 4in
　　　Width – 1.85m/6ft 1in
Armament: Main – 2cm/0.79in KwK30 gun, and coaxial 7.92mm/0.312in MG34 machine-gun
　　　Secondary – 7.92mm/0.312in MG34 machine-gun
Armour: Maximum – 8mm/0.315in
Powerplant: Daimler-Benz M09 6-cylinder 48kW/65hp petrol engine
Performance: Speed – 65kph/40mph
　　　Range – 250km/150 miles

Sd Kfz 231 Heavy Armoured Car 8 Rad

Almost as soon as the first six-wheeled armoured cars entered service, the expanding German Army realized that a better vehicle was needed and so development started in 1935. The new vehicle was to have eight wheels and a more powerful engine, based on the chassis of the Bussing-NAG 8x8 truck. The new car was given the same designation as the six-wheeled car except that 8 Rad (8-wheel) was added after the name.

This new armoured car was the most advanced cross-country vehicle at the time with a good road speed. However, the vehicle was very complex, the chassis was very complicated and the vehicle was very expensive and slow to produce. The eight-wheel drive and steering proved to be of great benefit in areas such as the Eastern Front and it was well able to cope with the Russian mud. In combat, the vehicle's most significant drawback was its height, which made it easier to observe from a distance. The engine was mounted in the rear of the vehicle and the rear deck was sloped to give a clear view from the rear driving position, allowing the car to be driven easily in reverse. Combat reports led to a number of changes to the design

in 1940, the main one being increased armour. Production started in 1937 and finished in 1942, by which time 1,235 had been built. It remained in service until the end of World War II.

The Sd Kfz 232 was the long-range radio version with extra radios fitted. A large frame aerial was fixed above the rear of the vehicle, while a small frame was fitted to the top of the turret with a pivot which allowed the turret freedom to traverse with the aerial attached.

The Sd Kfz 263 was a special command vehicle that had a fixed superstructure in place of the turret, extra radio sets and a large frame aerial, as in the Sd Kfz 232, attached to the top of the vehicle.

These vehicles came to prominence during the fighting in North Africa when they could range far and wide in the open expanses of the desert environment.

ABOVE: **A late production Sd Kfz 232 heavy radio car. This Sd Kfz 232 is fitted with a star aerial, which replaced the fixed frame aerial, attached to the rear of the car. The Sd Kfz 232 was fitted internally with extra radio equipment. The small rods at the front and rear of the vehicle help the driver judge the vehicle width.** BELOW: **A standard heavy Sd Kfz 231 armoured car. This car is fitted with an armoured shield on the front of the car, which had a secondary role as a storage bin. The hatch on the front of the vehicle gives access to the driver's controls.**
BOTTOM LEFT: **This is a fixed-frame Sd Kfz 232 radio car on active service in Poland in 1939. The additional armoured shield has not as yet been fitted to the vehicle. The white cross has been smeared with mud.**

Sd Kfz 231 Heavy Armoured Car 8 Rad

Country: Germany
Entered service: 1937
Crew: 4
Weight: 8,433kg/8.3 tons
Dimensions: Length – 5.85m/19ft 2in
    Height – 2.34m/7ft 8in
    Width – 2.2m/7ft 3in
Armament: Main – 2cm/0.79in KwK38 gun and
    coaxial 7.92mm/0.312in MG34 machine-gun
    Secondary – Small arms
Armour: Maximum – 30mm/1.18in
Powerplant: Bussing-NAG L8V-GS 8-cylinder
    112kW/150hp petrol engine
Performance: Speed – 85kph/53mph
    Range – 150km/95 miles

LEFT AND ABOVE: **The main gun is offset to the right of the vehicle and there is a large cut-out next to the driver to allow the weapon to fire directly forwards. The gunsight periscope can be seen above the gun shield on the driver's side.**

Sd Kfz 233 7.5cm Heavy Armoured Car 8 Rad

The Sd Kfz 233 was manufactured by F. Schichau in Elbing from December 1942 to October 1943 with a total production run of 119 vehicles. These vehicles were issued to armoured reconnaissance units of the German Army to increase the offensive power of the unit and to act as a close-support weapon.

The basic chassis of this vehicle was the same as the Sd Kfz 231 8 Rad heavy armoured car, but otherwise there were substantial differences between the two. The Sd Kfz 233 had the turret removed while the roof of the fighting compartment was cut away to allow the gun crew to man the main weapon, but they were very exposed as the sides of the vehicle gave them little protection

when standing up. On later models the height of the side walls of the fighting compartment were raised by 20mm/ 0.79in which gave the crew better protection, but the interior of the fighting compartment was very cramped as, apart from the gun and mount, there were 55 rounds of ammunition for the main armament. The front right-hand side of the original Sd Kfz 231 design was cut away to make room for the 7.5cm/2.95in KwK37 short-barrelled, low-velocity tank gun. This weapon was salvaged from Panzer III and Panzer IV tanks when both types had their main armament upgraded to a longer gun. It had very limited traverse, an elevation of only 12 degrees in every plane, and could fire high-

explosive and armour-piercing ammunition. The driver remained in the front of the vehicle, but was offset to the left-hand side to create space for the gun mount while the rear driving position was retained as before. The frontal armour of the vehicle was upgraded to 30mm/1.18in as a result of feedback from combat reports of early operations with the basic armoured car.

These vehicles first saw action with the *Afrika Korps* during the campaign in North Africa and were well-liked by their crews for their reliability and ruggedness. The Sd Kfz 233 served on all fronts during World War II.

Sd Kfz 233 7.5cm Heavy Armoured Car 8 Rad

Country: Germany
Entered service: 1942
Crew: 3
Weight: 8,839kg/8.7 tons
Dimensions: Length – 5.85m/19ft 2in
  Height – 2.25m/7ft 5in
  Width – 2.2m/7ft 2in
Armament: Main – 7.5cm/2.95in KwK37
  low-velocity gun
  Secondary – 7.92mm/0.312in MG34
  machine-gun
Armour: Maximum – 30mm/1.18in
Powerplant: Bussing-NAG L8V-GS 8-cylinder
  134kW/180hp petrol engine
Performance: Speed – 85kph/53mph
  Range – 300km/190 miles

ABOVE: **The top of this vehicle has been covered with a canvas sheet, which is supported on two curved frames. This vehicle is also fitted front and back with width indicators.**

Sd Kfz 234/2 Puma Heavy Armoured Car

In August 1940, the German Army issued a requirement for a new heavy armoured car. This was to have a monocoque hull, i.e. no chassis, the wheels and suspension being attached directly to the hull of the vehicle. The car was also to be fitted with a Tatra diesel engine that would be both more powerful and more suited to operating in hot climates. The new vehicle would have increased armoured protection, increased internal fuel capacity, and in general better performance than previous armoured cars. The new body design was given the designation ARK and production lasted from September 1943 to September 1944. The original order was for 1,500 vehicles but this was reduced to 100 when the Sd Kfz 234/1 (earlier number but later into production) came into service. The first Puma cars had a range of 600km/373 miles but by improving the fuel capacity this was increased to 1,000km/621 miles. These changes would make this car the best all-round vehicle in its class during World War II.

The turret of the Puma was originally designed for the cancelled Leopard light tank. It was of an oval design with steeply sloping sides, giving it an excellent ballistic shape, and there were two hatches in the roof. The main armament was fitted with a semi-automatic sliding breach and a hydro-pneumatic recoil system mounted above the gun. The barrel was terminated with a muzzle brake and the mantlet was a single piece casting known as a "Saukopf" (Sow's Head). The Puma was very similar in design to the Sd Kfz 231 but it had large single-piece side fenders with four built in storage boxes on each side.

The 100 Pumas were divided up into four units of 25 cars and sent to join four armoured regiments, with which they would see service on both the Eastern and Western Fronts. The superb Sd Kfz 234 series of cars were the only reconnaissance vehicles kept in production after March 1945 with 100 of the various marks being produced each month until the end of the war.

ABOVE: **This is an Sd Kfz 234/1 armoured car and uses the same chassis as the 234/2. In 1943 an order was given that 50 per cent of Sd Kfz 234 production was to be armed with the 2cm/0.79in KwK38. The top of the turret has been fitted with the wire-mesh anti-grenade screen.**

ABOVE: **This vehicle is fitted with a Saukopf gun mantlet, and there are three smoke dischargers on each side of the turret. The side panniers are now made in one piece and give more storage space.**

LEFT: **The exhaust for the car is mounted on the rear of the side pannier, just above the rear wheel. This car belonged to a Panzer Grenadier regiment in Normandy.**

Sd Kfz 234/2 5cm Puma Heavy Armoured Car

Country: Germany
Entered service: 1943
Crew: 4
Weight: 11,928kg/11.74 tons
Dimensions: Length – 6.8m/22ft 4in
    Height – 2.28m/7ft 6in
    Width – 2.4m/7ft 10in
Armament: Main – 5cm/1.97in KwK39/1
    anti-tank gun and coaxial 7.92mm/0.312in
    MG42 machine-gun
    Secondary – Small arms
Armour: Maximum – 30mm/1.18in
Powerplant: Tatra 103 12-cylinder 164kW/220hp
    diesel engine
Performance: Speed – 85kph/53mph
    Range – 1,000km/621 miles

Sd Kfz 234 7.5cm Heavy Support Armoured Cars

ABOVE LEFT: **The driver's position is now in the middle of the front of the car and the gun is mounted above the driver. The height of the armour has been increased to give the crew better protection.** ABOVE: **An Sd Kfz 234/4 armoured car armed with the PaK40 AT gun which went into production in December 1944.**

In September 1943, half of all the new Sd Kfz 234 chassis produced were ordered to be converted into support vehicles for the reconnaissance forces. These cars were to mount the 7.5cm/ 2.95in KwK37 to enable them to act as close-support vehicles. The KwK37 had been removed from the Panzer IV in 1942 when the tank was upgunned and these weapons had been placed into store until required, so this seemed a quick and easy way to give the reconnaissance force some real hitting power on the new chassis.

From June 1944, it was decided that only one in four vehicles would be converted in this way. Then in November 1944, Hitler ordered that the PaK40 should be fitted to these vehicles, turning them into self-propelled anti-tank

mounts. It was consequently often called the PaK-Wagen by the troops. In December 1944, production of the Sd Kfz 234/3 was stopped in favour of the new vehicle, the Sd Kfz 234/4, which would remain in production until March 1945. The Germans produced 88 of the Sd Kfz 234/3 and 89 of the Sd Kfz 234/4. The fighting compartment of both vehicles was open-topped but the sides were raised to give the crew some protection from small arms fire and shell splinters. The PaK40 was mounted on a pedestal mount and had limited traverse. It was raised up in the fighting compartment so that the driver could remain in his position under the gun in the centre of the front of the vehicle. One significant shortcoming with the Sd Kfz 234/4 was that it could only

carry 12 rounds of ammunition; the Sd Kfz 234/3 on the other hand carried 50 rounds of ammunition. The crew in both vehicles was increased from three to four, so that the driver was not necessary as part of the gun crew and could remain in position.

These heavy-support armoured cars were mainly issued to units in the West, but not always to the Panzer divisions. A number of these vehicles were sent to Normandy to help in attempting to stop the Allied invasion of France, but were easy prey for Allied aircraft.

LEFT: **The PaK40 takes up most of the room in the fighting compartment. It is mounted on a pedestal mount behind the driver and retains its original gun shield. The gun crew were very exposed when operating the gun.**

Sd Kfz 234/3 7.5cm Heavy Support Armoured Car

Country: Germany
Entered service: 1944
Crew: 4
Weight: 11,684kg/11.5 tons
Dimensions: Length – 6m/19ft 8in
   Height – 2.21m/7ft 3in
   Width – 2.4m/7ft 10in
Armament: Main – 7.5cm/2.95in KwK37 gun
   Secondary – 7.92mm/0.312in MG34 or
   MG42 machine-gun
Armour: Maximum – 30mm/1.2in
Powerplant: Tatra 103 12-cylinder 164kW/220hp
   diesel engine
Performance: Speed – 85kph/53mph
   Range – 1,000km/621 miles

LEFT AND ABOVE: **The Sd Kfz 251 on the left has the normal frontal armament of a single machine-gun, while the vehicle above has had the PaK35/36 fitted to increase the fire power of the half-track.**

Sd Kfz 251 Medium Half-Track

During the development of the Panzer Division in Germany throughout the 1930s it was very quickly realized that an armoured personnel carrier would be required and that this would have to have good cross-country ability to keep pace with the tanks. Development of a suitable vehicle started in 1937 with Hanomag producing the chassis and Bussing-NAG building the body. Production started in 1939 and initially three marks, A, B, and C, were built with 4,650 vehicles produced in total, but by far the largest production run was of the Ausf D of which 10,602 were built. This mark would remain in production until the end of World War II. General Guderian was unhappy with the original design as he anticipated that the Panzer Grenadiers would occasionally have to fight from inside their vehicles making the large open top a great weakness.

ABOVE: **This knocked-out Sd Kfz 251 Ausf D is a late version and has its engine covers in the open position.**

The chassis of the Sd Kfz 251 was very strong and well-protected and this gave the whole vehicle great strength. The body of the vehicle was bolted to the chassis in the early marks and was made in two sections with each section being bolted together just behind the driver's position. The body of Ausf A, B and C had a good ballistic shape but were very difficult and slow to produce. Hanomag and Bussing-NAG could not keep up with demand so other manufacturers were brought in to speed up production. The engine was at the front with the driver and commander's position behind and this area had an armoured roof on which a machine-gun was mounted. The platoon commander's vehicle would have a 3.7cm/1.46in anti-tank gun mounted on the roof instead of the machine-gun. The infantry section sat in the back on two benches running the length of the rear area with the men facing inwards. Two large doors giving easy accessibility for the infantry section were positioned at the rear, and above these was a mount for an anti-aircraft machine-gun. There were no brakes fitted to the front wheels; these were fitted instead to the driving sprockets of the track section. The tracks were light and lubricated, and each track shoe was fitted with a rubber pad which helped prolong the track life of the vehicle. Each road wheel had a rubber tyre and was grouped in a pair, being supported on a torsion bar type suspension system.

The last type of the Sd Kfz 251 was the Ausf D. This went into production in 1944 and was a major redesign of the basic vehicle. The Ausf D had a greatly simplified construction with the use of larger flat armour plates to build the body, which was now of an all-welded construction. The rear door was built with a reverse slope and the storage boxes along the sides had become part of the main body of the vehicle.

LEFT: **This German vehicle is symbolic of Blitzkrieg and would remain in service with other countries for many years after the war. The Sd Kfz 251 Ausf A has a large number of angled plates and this made production slow. Three storage bins are fitted on each side of the vehicle between the top of the tracks and the body of the vehicle.**

There were no less than 22 official variations of the basic half-track design. Many were simply changes in the armament fitted to the vehicle while others included command, communications, ambulance and observation types. The most powerful variant of these vehicles was the Sd Kfz 251/1 *Stuka zum Fuss* (Dive-bomber on Foot) which was more commonly known as the Infantry Stuka. Racks were fitted to the sides of the vehicle and three 28cm/11in or 32cm/12.6in rockets, which could be fitted with either high-explosive or incendiary warheads, could be mounted on each side. They were used to demolish strongpoints or large structures and also to give support to an attack on an enemy position. The last version was the Sd Kfz 251/22 which mounted the PaK40 7.5cm/2.95in anti-tank gun. However, the sheer weight of the weapon overloaded the half-track and firing the gun also put a great strain on the suspension of the vehicle.

Skoda in Czechoslovakia was one of the manufacturers of the Sd Kfz 251 and it was decided after World War II to keep it in production for the Czechoslovakian Army as the firm was tooled up to build this vehicle. With this second lease of life the vehicle would remain in service until 1980.

ABOVE: **This picture clearly shows the low profile of the Sd Kfz 251 Ausf A. To increase the frontal armour of the vehicle a common practice was to attach spare track-link to the front.** LEFT: **This is the post-war version of the Sd Kfz 251 that continued to be made in Czechoslovakia after World War II. This vehicle was known as the OT-810 and would remain in service for many years.**

Sd Kfz 251/1 Ausf A Medium Half-Track

Country: Germany
Entered service: 1939
Crew: 2 plus 10 infantry
Weight: 7,935kg/7.81 tons
Dimensions: Length – 5.8m/19ft
  Height – 1.75m/5ft 9in
  Width – 2.1m/6ft 10in
Armament: Main – 2 x 7.92mm/0.312in MG34
  machine-guns
  Secondary – Small arms
Armour: Maximum – 15mm/0.59in
Powerplant: Maybach HL42 TUKRM 6-cylinder
  89kW/120hp petrol engine
Performance: Speed – 53kph/33mph
  Range – 300km/185 miles

Sd Kfz 250 Half–Track Armoured Personnel Carrier

This vehicle had its roots in the operational requirements of the German Army in the mid-1930s which led to the manufacture of the Sd Kfz 251 3,048kg/3-ton half-track. The Sd Kfz 250 was produced by two companies; the Demag AG Company of Wetter in the Ruhr built the chassis while Bussing-NAG built the body of the vehicle. There was a total production run of 5,930 of these carriers, which were designed to transport a half-section of infantry in support of the reconnaissance units. Trials started in 1939 and although delays held up production until 1940, a number of these vehicles were in service with the German Army by the time of the invasion of France.

The Sd Kfz 250 was an open-topped vehicle which could carry five men and a driver. In the rear of the vehicle was a single door, which made debussing slow. The front wheels were not powered and so made steering heavy. When a sharp turn was made using the steering wheel,

this action would automatically engage the required track-brake and so help the vehicle make the sharp turn. Two other variations were being built at the same time as the basic vehicle. The first was an ammunition carrier for the StuG batteries while the other vehicle was a signals car that could carry two large radios and had a large frame aerial over the top. In 1943, the Sd Kfz 250 was completely redesigned to make production simpler and faster. The angled sides of the crew compartment were now flattened and made from a single piece of armour plate.

These half-tracks were built in 15 official variants and many other modifications were carried out by vehicle crews in the field. In one variant, an armoured cover was fitted over the crew compartment and a turret placed on top. These vehicles replaced the 4x4 Sd Kfz 222 armoured car in front-line service. Among the other variants there were a mortar carrier, a telephone exchange, an ammunition carrier, a command car and a self-propelled gun mount. These vehicles would remain in service until the end of World War II.

ABOVE: **This Sd Kfz 250 is "under new ownership" as it is being driven by British soldiers. Half the gun shield is missing along with the machine-gun. The half-track is passing over a pontoon bridge.**

LEFT: **This Sd Kfz 250 half-track is on active service in the desert of North Africa. It has had its forward firepower increased by the fitting of a PaK35/36.**

RIGHT: **This vehicle replaced the Sd Kfz 222 wheeled armoured car in service. The rear of the vehicle was roofed over and the turret from the armoured car was placed into the roof of the half-track. This vehicle has a crew of three and would remain in service until 1945.**

Sd Kfz 250/1 Half-Track Armoured Personnel Carrier

Country: Germany
Entered service: 1940
Crew: 1 plus 5 infantry
Weight: 5,893kg/5.8 tons
Dimensions: Length – 4.56m/15ft
    Height – 1.98m/6ft 6in
    Width – 1.95m/6ft 5in
Armament: Main – 2 x 7.92mm/0.312in MG34
    machine-gun
    Secondary – Small arms
Armour: Maximum – 14.5mm/0.57in
Powerplant: Maybach HL42 6-cylinder
    74.6kW/100hp petrol engine
Performance: Speed – 59.5kph/37mph
    Range – 299km/186 miles

LEFT: **This vehicle uses the M40 chassis which was the first type used. The main visual difference between the two chassis is that the track-guard does not run the length of the vehicle in the M40.**
ABOVE: **This SPG uses the M42 chassis and was the final version of this vehicle. The gun has a very distinctive "pepper-pot" muzzle brake.**

Semovente M42 DA 75/18 Self-Propelled Gun

This was an excellent self-propelled gun/howitzer and was the first Italian vehicle to be produced as part of a series during World War II. The M42 was tested in early 1941 and went into production the same year with the first vehicles being issued to service units later that year. The first unit to receive these new vehicles was the Ariete Division who initially used it in North Africa in early 1942. Originally intended to fulfil a self-propelled artillery role within the armoured division, they were more often deployed in an anti-tank role. At this time, these vehicles were the best armed self-propelled guns in North Africa and could easily outgun any British or German tank.

The first vehicles in this series were built on the M13/40 tank chassis, but later the chassis of the M14/41 was used, with production being stopped in 1943. The first order was for 200 vehicles and this was met in full, with a further order for 500 being placed in 1943. These new vehicles were to be equipped with the 75/34, a longer gun. The M42 could carry 100 rounds of 75mm/2.95in

ammunition. However, delays in putting the new P40 tank into production resulted in the unused guns being fitted to the M42, which then became the M42M. None of these vehicles were issued to the Italian Army before Italy's surrender but they were captured and used by the Germans.

Each M42 battery was given a command vehicle built on the M13/40 chassis. This was basically a turretless tank chassis that was initially armed with twin 8mm/0.315in machine-guns mounted on the right-hand side of the vehicle. The twin guns were later replaced by a single 13.5mm/0.53in heavy machine-gun.

When Italy surrendered in 1943, the Germans took over the production facilities for the M42 as they had found this vehicle to be very good. They also took 292 of them into German service, common practice with captured weapons they admired. These vehicles would see constant service during 1944 in Italy and the Balkans and by January 1945 only 93 were left in action after months of heavy fighting.

ABOVE: **The driver's position in the Semovente M42. The side of the main armament sits beside the driver's head. The large lever in the picture is the firing handle.**

Semovente M42 DA 75/18 SPG

Country: Italy
Entered service: 1942
Crew: 3
Weight: 15,240kg/15 tons
Dimensions: Length – 5.04m/16ft 6in
    Height – 1.85m/6ft 1in
    Width – 2.23m/7ft 4in
Armament: Main – 75mm/2.95in model 35
    gun/howitzer
    Secondary – 8mm/0.315in Breda model 38
Armour: Maximum – 50mm/1.97in
Powerplant: Spa 15 TM41 8-cylinder
    138kW/185hp petrol engine
Performance: Speed – 38kph/24mph
    Range – 230km/143 miles

LEFT: **The Canadian Ram tank was used for this conversion. The Ram was a right-hand-drive vehicle and so the British crews took to it quickly. The driver's hatch on this vehicle is in the open position. The fighting compartment is covered with a canvas roof giving the crew some protection from the weather.**

Sexton 25pdr Self-Propelled Gun

In 1942, the Americans attempted to improve the M7 Priest by replacing the existing armament with a British 25pdr gun. The "pulpit" was retained to give the vehicle some close-quarter protection, and the gun was mounted well over on the right-hand side of the fighting compartment. There were a number of delays in the development programme when the first live-firing of the gun destroyed the gun mount. By the time the vehicle was ready for a second test firing, the Canadians had come up with the Sexton and so in March 1943 the British cancelled the American project in favour of the simpler Canadian vehicle.

The Canadian Department of National Defence selected the Ram tank to act as a chassis for the 25pdr gun to meet the British Army requirement for a self-propelled gun. The pilot model was finished in late 1942 and it proved to be very successful in tests. Production started at the Montreal Locomotive Works in early 1943 and continued until 1945, by which time 2,150 had been built. Originally designated the "25-pounder Ram Carrier", it was renamed following Royal Artillery tradition and given the religious name "Sexton". The 25pdr was mounted just off the centreline to the left-hand side of the fighting compartment. The driver's position was on the right-

LEFT AND RIGHT: **The driver's position in the vehicle is very cramped and yet very light, as it is open at the top into the fighting compartment. The dashboard has the minimum of gauges, and in the centre are the track control levers. The large doors on the rear of the vehicle give access to the radial engine.**

hand side of the fighting compartment down in the bottom of the tank chassis, the driver being below the level of the gun. The fighting compartment was constructed out of 12mm/0.47in armour plate, with an open back and low sides extending to just above waist height. It was also open-topped and exposed to the elements. However, a number of Sexton batteries had steel loops made in field workshops so that a canvas cover or tent could be placed over the fighting compartment. The front of the fighting compartment was protected by 25mm/0.98in armour plate with the final drive housing being in three pieces that were bolted together.

The 25pdr gun had a traverse of 25 degrees to the left and 15 degrees to the right, while the elevation range was plus 40 degrees to minus 9 degrees. The recoil of the gun was also restricted to 51cm/1ft 8in compared with 91cm/3ft of the standard 25pdr. The main ammunition storage was under the floor of the fighting compartment and held 112 rounds, but there was also one small ready-to-use locker on the rear wall of the fighting compartment. On a later version of the Sexton this housing was changed to a single casting and the running gear was modified. The suspension system was also changed on the Sexton II from an M3 style to an M4 trailing arm type, and the Canadian dry pin track was used. The rear deck of the vehicle carried box structures in each corner for batteries and an auxiliary generator.

The first 124 vehicles produced were designated Sexton I, but following a number of modifications the improved vehicle became the Sexton II. The Sexton I had no provision for anti-aircraft machine-guns on the vehicle and this was addressed with the Sexton II with the addition of two Bren light machine-guns. A number of Sextons also had a 12.7mm/50cal machine-gun fitted to the front left-hand corner of the fighting compartment as a field modification.

Some Sextons were converted to Gun Position Officers (GPO) vehicles with one of these being issued to each Sexton battery. This conversion involved the removal of the gun and most of the internal fittings to provide space for a map table, extra field telephones, and radios.

The Sexton would become the standard medium self-propelled gun used by the British and Canadian armies in World War II. It first saw action with the 8th Army in Italy and was used throughout the campaign in northern Europe. Some British units that were converted from the Priest to the Sexton had very few days to practise with their new equipment before going into action on June 6, 1944. A number of Sexton units were allocated "run-in shooting" missions (firing at shore targets from the landing craft bringing them in) as they landed on the D-Day beaches. This was intended to aid in the suppression of the German beach defences but, perhaps not surprisingly, was not very accurate.

ABOVE: **This Sexton has had an additional machine-gun fitted to the front of the fighting compartment above the driver. The front of the vehicle is three separate pieces bolted together. This gun has been assigned to the 11th Armoured Division.** BELOW: **The main weapon of the Sexton is the British 25pdr gun. The breach of this weapon slides vertically and the red wheels are the elevation and traverse controls.**

Sexton 25pdr SPG

Country: Canada
Entered service: 1942
Crew: 6
Weight: 25,908kg/25.5 tons
Dimensions: Length – 6.12m/20ft 1in
  Height – 2.43m/8ft
  Width – 2.71m/8ft 11in
Armament: Main – 11kg/25pdr C Mk II or III
  Secondary – 2 x 7.7mm/0.303in Bren
  light machine-gun
Armour: Maximum – 32mm/1.26in
Powerplant: Continental 9-cylinder 298kW/400hp
  radial petrol engine
Performance: Speed – 38kph/24mph
  Range – 200km/125 miles

LEFT: **The height of this vehicle is very apparent and led to a number of problems during combat. The driver's position is on the left-hand side of the vehicle. These SPGs were issued to six Panzer divisions in 1940.** BELOW: **The gun and its unaltered carriage were placed on to the top of the Panzer I. The open rear and open top of the gun shield give the crew very little protection from either the weather or small-arms fire.**

sIG33 15cm Infantry Support Self-Propelled Gun

This was the first self-propelled gun to see service in the German Army of World War II, and valuable experience was gained from its combat performance. It was an improvised vehicle manufactured to an army specification for a fully tracked vehicle that could give close support to the infantry. These vehicles were built by Alkett in 1939 and entered service in time to take part in the Blitzkrieg operation throughout northern France and the Low Countries in 1940. While it represented a great step forward for the military, it had significant faults and only 38 of these vehicles were built.

The chassis was that of the Panzer I Ausf B with the turret removed and the superstructure left in place. At this time,

the Panzer I was already being replaced by bigger and better tanks thus providing the chassis to mount the sIG33. A large box structure, 1.83m/6ft in height constructed of 10mm/0.394in armour was built on the vehicle. This box was open-topped, with two small doors on the rear which did not meet in the middle but only partially closed the opening. The gun, which retained its wheels and box trail, was mounted inside the box on the top of the tank superstructure.

This SPG could be brought into action very quickly and open fire instantly. It also proved to be very efficient in service. However, it is worth considering that all infantry guns were horse-drawn until this vehicle made its appearance, and so it did not have any equivalent competition.

The vehicle was not designated an Sd Kfz number and had a number of major faults. At over 2.74m/9ft high, the vehicle was very tall which gave it a high centre of gravity. It was also overloaded which placed a great strain on the suspension and contributed to the poor cross-country ability.

These guns were issued to Heavy Infantry Gun Companies 701–706, in early 1940. They would remain in service until 1943 when the last unit, the 704th of the 5th Panzer Division, was refitted.

LEFT: **An improved mount for the sIG 15cm was built using the Panzer II chassis. An extra road wheel had to be fitted to each side of the vehicle, which had been widened and lengthened. Only 12 of these vehicles were built and all were sent to the *Afrika Korps* in North Africa.**

sIG33 15cm Infantry Support SPG

Country: Germany
Entered service: 1940
Crew: 4
Weight: 8,636kg/8.5 tons
Dimensions: Length – 4.42m/14ft 6in
Height – 3.35m/11ft
Width – 2.6m/8ft 6in
Armament: Main – 15cm/5.91in sIG33 L/11 gun
Secondary – Small arms
Armour: Maximum – 13mm/0.51in
Powerplant: Maybach NL38 TKRM 6-cylinder
75kW/100hp petrol engine
Performance: Speed – 40kph/25mph
Range – 140km/87 miles

LEFT: **This Staghound has both the driver's and hull gunner's front hatches in the open position. The side hatch behind the front wheel is also open and gives direct access to the driver's position. The large drum on the side of the vehicle is a fuel tank.**

ABOVE: **British Staghound armoured cars moving along an old railway line. The tyres of the cars have been fitted with "snow chains" to help them move across the soft ground in the winter. These cars remained in British service well after World War II.**

BELOW LEFT: **This is the close-support version of the Staghound and was armed with a short 76.2mm/ 3in howitzer.**

Staghound Armoured Car

The Staghound was an American designed and built vehicle that was destined never to be used by the US Army. All the cars of this type that were produced were sent to the British and Commonwealth armies. The design had its origins in a US Army requirement for a heavy armoured car, which was developed in two forms – one with six wheels (T17) and one with four wheels (T17E1). The British Tank Mission to America saw the two cars, which had been heavily influenced by British experience in battle, selected the T17E1 and placed an initial order for 300 vehicles. Production started in early 1942 with the first vehicles entering service in later the same year. In British service, the vehicle was called the Staghound Mk I.

The Staghound was a large well-armoured vehicle having a 37mm/

1.46in gun and coaxial 7.62mm/0.3in machine-gun in the turret. In combat it proved to be very reliable, easy to maintain and had good cross-country ability. It had a fully automatic hydraulic transmission with two engines mounted side by side in the rear of the vehicle, and two 173-litre/38-gallon jettison fuel tanks to increase the vehicle's range. The vehicle had no chassis with the suspension parts attaching directly to the hull. Two further machine-guns were fitted to the vehicle, one in the front next to the driver and one on a pintle mount on the rear of the turret for anti-aircraft use. However, the Staghound was found to be too large, heavy and unwieldy for fighting in northern Europe and Italy compared to the British Daimler armoured car and was not well-liked by its British and Commonwealth crews.

The British were to produce three more versions of the Staghound. The Mk II was a close-support version with a short 75mm/ 2.95in gun mounted in a new turret. The Mk III was an attempt to upgun the Staghound by fitting the Crusader III 75mm/2.95in gun turret to the vehicle, turning it into a wheeled tank. The last conversion was the Staghound AA vehicle, armed with two 12.7mm/0.5in machine-guns in a small open-topped turret. None of these conversions was produced in large numbers.

Staghound Mk I Armoured Car	
Country: USA	
Entered service: 1942	
Crew: 5	
Weight: 14,122kg/13.9 tons	
Dimensions: Length – 5.49m/18ft	
Height – 2.36m/7ft 9in	
Width – 2.69m/8ft 10in	
Armament: Main – 37mm/1.46in ATG,	
and coaxial 7.62mm/0.3in machine-gun	
Secondary – 2 x 7.62mm/0.3in machine-guns	
Armour: Maximum – 22mm/0.866in	
Powerplant: 2 x GMC 270 6-cylinder 72kW/97hp	
petrol engine	
Performance: Speed – 89kph/55mph	
Range – 724km/450 miles	

Sturmgeschutz III Self-Propelled Gun

The Sturmgeschutz III (StuG III) was an excellent vehicle performing well as a close-support weapon and, with its ability to take larger guns, would remain in service for most of World War II. It was relatively cheap and easy to produce when compared with a tank and this proved to be important in wartime Germany. Towards the end of the war, the StuG III would also have to fill gaps left by the shortage of tanks in the Panzer divisions – a role for which it was never designed – and was without doubt one of the most important vehicles the Germans produced in World War II.

The order to develop a close-support vehicle was given in June 1937 and by January 1940 the resulting vehicle was placed into production and given the designation of StuG III Ausf A. Two companies, Alkett and MIAG, undertook most of the production but these would be joined by MAN at times when extra output capacity was required. It used the same chassis, suspension and engine as the Panzer III Ausf F. The upper hull and turret were removed and replaced with a thick carapace of armour. A short 7.5cm/2.95in gun was mounted in the front of the vehicle and offset to the right providing space for the driver who sat on the left next to the main armament. These basic positions would not change throughout its career, even after a number of improvements. The Ausf B had improvements to the engine while Ausf C and D had improvements to the superstructure of the fighting compartment. The Ausf E was the last of the short-barrelled StuG IIIs and it was the first model to have a close-support machine-gun fitted to the upper hull. The standard gun up until then had been the 7.5cm/2.95in L/24 gun (the length of the barrel was 24 times the calibre).

TOP: **This was the most numerous StuG produced during World War II. The vehicle was made up of the Panzer III chassis and running gear. The superstructure was in two parts, with the main armament trunnioned between. The shield on the roof of the vehicle is for the close-support machine-gun.**
ABOVE: **The travel lock is mounted on the front of the vehicle under the gun barrel. When the vehicle was travelling any distance the barrel would be locked in place to save the gun mounting from damage.**

From April 1942 onwards when the Ausf F entered service, the gun length increased to L/43, and this was further improved in June when the gun was changed to the L/48. This gave the StuG III a very potent anti-tank capability that would serve the vehicle well for the remainder of the war.

The last version of the StuG III was the Ausf G that entered service in January 1943 and would remain in production and active service until the end of the war. The Ausf G had a number of improvements to the superstructure, such as the addition of a commander's cupola with periscopes and sloping of the side plates. Other modifications were the introduction of the *Saukopf* (Sow's Head) gun mantlet in late 1943, and the

LEFT: **The front of the fighting compartment had extra armour bolted to it, as on the left-hand side of the picture. In the middle is the gun mantlet and on the right is the driver's vision slit.** ABOVE: **This StuG III has had several bolt-on plates added to the front of the vehicle to increase its armour thickness.**

LEFT: **Two British soldiers are looking at the hits on this StuG III which has been struck four times on the lower front hull plate. The gun mantlet has collapsed into the vehicle.**

addition of a coaxial machine-gun in early 1944 as these vehicles were now engaging enemy infantry at close-quarters.

Variants of the StuG III included an assault howitzer which mounted a 10.5cm/4.13in gun for close-support duties. Alkett manufactured a total of 1,211 of these vehicles from October 1942 to March 1945.

From 1943 onwards, the StuG III was fitted with two further defensive measures. February 1943 saw the introduction of *Schürzen* (skirts). Made from wire mesh or metal plates, these helped stop anti-tank shells from penetrating the side of the vehicle where the armour was thin. However, the procurement of wire mesh proved difficult and so side-skirts of this type were not produced in great numbers. The second defensive measure was the introduction of *Zimmerit*. This was

a protective coating, 3–5mm/0.1–0.2in thick, that covered the hull and superstructure and was intended to prevent Russian troops from attaching magnetic mines or shaped charges to the hull of the vehicle. Initially this coating was to be made of tar but AFV crews rejected this due to the fire hazard, so a thin layer of cement paste was put on the vehicle instead, giving it a very distinctive finish.

During World War II, 74 StuG units were formed and these saw active service on all fronts. Total war production was 10,306 Sturmgeschutz III vehicles.

ABOVE: **This is one of the first StuG III prototype vehicles to enter service and has an open-topped fighting compartment. The vehicle is armed with the short 75cm/2.95in gun.**

Sturmgeschutz III SPG Ausf G

Country: Germany
Entered service: January 1943
Crew: 4
Weight: 24,282kg/23.9 tons
Dimensions: Length – 6.77m/22ft 3in
    Height – 2.16m/7ft 1in
    Width – 2.95m/9ft 8in
Armament: Main – 7.5cm/2.95in StuK40
    L/48 gun
    Secondary – 2 x 7.92mm/0.312in MG42
    machine-guns
Armour: Maximum – 80mm/3.15in
Powerplant: Maybach HL 120 TRM 12-cylinder
    197.6kW/265hp petrol engine
Performance: Speed – 40kph/24.9mph
    Range – 165km/102 miles

Sturmgeschutz IV Self-Propelled Gun

In February 1943, the Krupp company was asked to look at a proposal for mounting the StuG III superstructure on the Panzer IV chassis (8 BW). However, instead of using a basic Panzer IV chassis Krupp used a new development, the 9 BW chassis, which would have sloped frontal armour and much thicker side armour. These alterations would cause great disruption to StuG and Panzer IV production lines and resulted in no great saving in either the weight or the materials used in the new vehicle. These disruptions were deemed intolerable at this time, the spring of 1943, as the war was showing signs of turning against Germany.

In late November 1943, the Alkett factory was badly damaged during a bombing raid and production of the StuG III suffered. Hitler insisted that the shortfall must be made up and therefore some of the Panzer IV facilities at the Krupp factory in Magdeburg were reassigned to the production of a StuG IV using StuG III superstructures. The new StuG IV was shown to

ABOVE LEFT: **A column of StuG IVs stopped in the road. The vehicles are all fitted with the Saukopf mantle, and are carrying spare road wheels on the side of the vehicle.** ABOVE: **The front of this StuG has been covered with various lengths of spare track.**

Hitler on December 16, 1943, and he approved the vehicle, insisting that it was put into production immediately. An additional impetus was provided by combat reports stating that the Panzer IV was having a hard time on the battlefield, and the losses from battles such as Kursk also had to be made up as quickly as possible.

The Panzer IV chassis was combined with the superstructure of the StuG III G but due to the greater length of the tank, the driver's compartment was positioned forward of the superstructure and a special armoured cupola was built for the driver. This box-shaped structure was situated on the left-hand side at the front of the vehicle, with two periscopes

LEFT: **This vehicle has been fitted with rails for the side-skirt armour. The body of the SPG has been covered in anti-magnetic *Zimmerit* paste. On the roof of the vehicle is a remote-controlled close-support machine-gun which is operated from inside the vehicle by one of the gun crew. The rail on the hull front is for spare track.**

mounted on top of the cupola along with an escape hatch. The Panzer IV escape hatch was in the belly of the vehicle for use by the driver and radio operator, but in the StuG IV this was welded shut as it was not required. Ammunition storage was 87 rounds; an additional 12-round bin was planned for the engine bay utilizing vacant space left by the unfitted turret motors. However, this caused problems and at times great confusion at the chassis production plants so the idea was dropped. The StuG IV was also to be fitted with concrete armour. The concrete was to be applied some 100mm/3.9in thick, mainly to the driver's position and the flat front on the right-hand side of the superstructure, but tests revealed that this did not help deflect incoming munitions and it added considerable weight to the vehicle. The modification was therefore stopped by the manufacturers, who simply put a coat of *Zimmerit* on the vehicle. However, the troops in the field thought it was a good idea and so added the concrete and extra armour plate to what they felt were weak areas. The driver's seat was adjustable and the back rest could be folded down so that the driver could escape into the fighting compartment if necessary. A 2,032kg/2-ton crane could be attached to the hull of the vehicle to ease the removal of the gun and could also be used for basic engine maintenance. The StuG IV was also fitted with the new Rundum-Feuer machine-gun, which could be operated from inside the vehicle and give all-round defence against attacking enemy infantry. Like with the StuG III, the StuG IV was fitted with *Schürzen* (skirts). These had been inspected by Hitler in March 1943 and were placed in to production immediately with the first field modification kits going out in early June 1943 to be fitted by field workshops.

The Sturmgeschutz was intended to act as close support for the infantry, but this was one role that the StuG IV would not perform as the bulk of these vehicles went either to Panzerjager units to act as tank destroyers or to Panzer Divisions as replacements for knocked-out tanks. In total, 1,141 StuG IVs were built by Krupp.

ABOVE: **This StuG IV has the side-skirts fitted. These acted as a form of spaced armour. The driver's position on the StuG IV was moved forward of the superstructure.** BELOW: **A close-up of the driver's cupola: the driver's hatch is in the open position. The vehicle commander's hatch is also open and the cut-out for the commander's periscope can be seen. The front of the driver's position has a thick layer of concrete which acts as additional armour.**

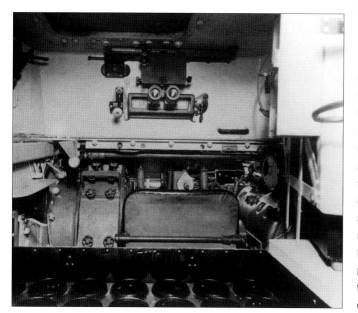

LEFT: **The driver's position inside a StuG IV. The periscope can be seen in front of the driver's seat. Above in the roof is the driver's hatch. The driving instruments are mounted on the right-hand side. In the front of the picture is one of the ammunition containers.**

Sturmgeschutz IV SPG	

Country: Germany
Entered service: 1944
Crew: 4
Weight: 23,368kg/23 tons
Dimensions: Length – 6.7m/22ft
 Height – 2.2m/7ft 3in
 Width – 2.95m/9ft 8in
Armament: Main – 7.5cm/2.95in StuK40 L/48 gun
 Secondary – 2 x 7.92mm/0.312in MG42 machine-guns
Armour: Maximum – 80mm/3.15in
Powerplant: Maybach HL 120 TRM 12-cylinder 198kW/265hp petrol engine
Performance: Speed – 38kph/24mph
 Range – 210km/131 miles

LEFT: **The hull of this Sturmmörser Tiger has been covered in** *Zimmerit*, **while the new superstructure and glacis are in painted bare metal. The crane on the rear of the fighting compartment is for loading the ammunition.** ABOVE: **Inside the rear of the fighting compartment is the ammunition storage. Six rounds were stored on each side of the loading tray. Due to the weight of the rounds, they were placed on the loading tray before being pushed up and into the weapon.**

Sturmmörser Tiger Assault Rocket Mortar

The Sturm Tiger was the largest of the German heavy self-propelled guns produced during World War II. Officially these vehicles were known as *38cm Raketenwerfer 61 auf Sturmmörser Tiger* (38cm Rocket Launcher 61 on Assault Mortar Tiger). They were never issued with an Sd Kfz number and only 18 of them were built by their manufacturer, Alkett.

The project originally arose out of a requirement from Hitler in August 1943 to mount the 21cm heavy-support gun, but this was changed when the 38cm launcher became available and could be mounted on a Tiger 1 chassis. Hitler felt that there would be a great demand from the troops in the front line for these vehicles. The inspiration came from battle experience gained at Stalingrad and Leningrad, where there was a requirement for heavy close-support vehicles. Hitler and Guderian agreed for one prototype to be built, with, if successful, a production run of ten vehicles per month. The prototype was demonstrated to Hitler in October 1943, and in April 1944 it was decided to start a limited production run of a dozen vehicles, launchers and superstructures.

The vehicle conversions were carried out by Alkett at their Berlin/Spandau works. By September 1944, the first seven vehicles had been finished with the total rising to 18 vehicles by the end of the year. The monthly output of 38cm rockets was envisaged to be 300 rounds, this weapon having originally been developed for the German Navy as an anti-submarine warfare system. Two different warheads were available, one being high-explosive and the other being a hollow charge. The complete round which weighed 329kg/726lb was 1.5m/5ft long, and was loaded on to the vehicle using a hand-operated crane mounted on the rear of the superstructure. The ceiling of

ABOVE: **A German Bergepanther is being used to move this Sturmmörser Tiger. The enormous size of the vehicle can be seen from the two British officers standing next to the vehicle.**

the vehicle was fitted with an overhead hoist to move the ammunition from its racks and on to a loading tray, a ram was used to load the weapon and then the loading tray was folded away so the weapon could be fired. There was storage for 12 rounds in the fighting compartment and a thirteenth was carried loaded in the mortar.

The conversion of the vehicle consisted of removing the turret and hull top of the Tiger from the engine compartment forward. The new fighting compartment made from sloping armour plate was placed over the open space. The front glacis plate was sloped at 45 degrees and was 150mm/5.91in thick, with the driver's vision block on the left side with a sighting

LEFT: **On the left of the picture is the close-support machine-gun blister. Above the driver's vision slit is the sighting aperture for the main weapon.**
ABOVE: **Inside the fighting compartment. A round has been placed in the weapon and the breach is about to be closed. The circle of small holes on the rear of the round is the rocket motor exhausts.**

aperture above it and a close-support machine-gun on the right. The side and rear plates were made of 80mm/3.15in armour with a circular hatch in the rear wall of the fighting compartment and a large loading door for the ammunition in the roof.

The rocket launcher was the most interesting part of this vehicle. It was breech-loaded and the barrel was rifled with a right-hand twist to induce spin into the munitions as they left the weapon. As the munitions were rocket-propelled, a way had to be found of stopping the rockets' exhaust from entering the fighting compartment. The exhaust gases operated a bypass valve in the breech which allowed the gases to escape forwards as the round left the barrel. The vehicle had to carry out "shoot and scoot" operations as the exhaust from the weapon was a give-away of the position of the vehicle even at the maximum range of 6km/3.7 miles.

As these vehicles could only carry a few rounds, each gun vehicle had to be supported by a tracked ammunition carrier built on Tiger 1 chassis that would carry an extra 40 rounds. Only one vehicle was ever produced before the Alkett factory was overrun by the Soviet Army.

Eighteen chassis were completed but only 12 of these vehicles were finished to be used in combat and these were formed into three companies of four vehicles each. The companies were 1001, 1002 and 1003, and were all used in the defence of the homeland, a task for which they were ill-suited. Some of them were used during the destruction of Warsaw and in fighting in other large cities.

ABOVE: **The small square blocks on the end of the barrel are for the attachment of a counterweight. On the top of the fighting compartment is a dome-shaped fume extractor.**

Sturmmörser Tiger Assault Rocket Mortar

Country: Germany
Entered service: 1944
Crew: 5
Weight: 66,040kg/65 tons
Dimensions: Length – 6.28m/20ft 7in
    Height – 2.85m/9ft 4in
    Width – 3.57m/11ft 9in
Armament: Main – 38cm/14.96in Stu M RW61 L/5.4 rocket motar
    Secondary – 7.92mm/0.312in MG42 machine-gun
Armour: Maximum – 150mm/5.91in
Powerplant: Maybach HL 230 P45 12-cylinder 522kW/700hp petrol engine
Performance: Speed – 40kph/25mph
    Range – 120km/75 miles

LEFT: **Several batteries of SU-76 vehicles drawn up for inspection. Part of the exhaust system can be seen below the vehicle number. This vehicle has had at least one tank kill, as it is painted on the side of the fighting compartment.** BELOW: **The very small fighting compartment can be clearly seen. The gunner is on the left, loader in the middle and vehicle commander on the right. The driver remained in his position in the front of the vehicle.**

SU-76 Self-Propelled Gun

In 1942, the task of developing a new self-propelled gun was given to the Kolomenskiy Locomotive Works in Kirov. They were instructed to mount the ZiS 3 76.2mm/3in gun on a suitable chassis. Initially the T-60 was selected for this project but this proved to be far too small. In the spring of 1942 it was decided that the longer, T-70 chassis was more suitable for the ZiS 3, and the improved new vehicle was called the SU-76. The T-70 was becoming available at this time because it was being phased out as a tank as it was too lightly armoured and the twin-engine layout, one for each track, was not reliable.

Trials were conducted in the summer of 1942 and the new vehicle went into production in December, 26 of these being built in that month and issued to the army, who found it to be unusable.

In early 1943 the vehicle was passed to a new design bureau, which made several changes. They placed the engines in-line so that power from both was fed to both tracks and consequently if an engine broke down the vehicle would not simply go round in circles. The new engine layout also required the front of the vehicle to be redesigned, and the fighting compartment was improved. This new vehicle was called the SU-76M.

Even in its improved version the SU-76 was never liked by the crews who had to use the vehicle. The fighting compartment was open-topped and gave the gun crew very little protection from small arms fire and no protection from the weather. The driver had to sit with the engines as there was no bulkhead separating the two compartments and the noise was horrendous, added to

which the heat was very hard to work with in the summer. These SPGs were originally designed as anti-tank vehicles but were soon relegated to an infantry-support role. Nevertheless, they would serve on into the 1960s, seeing action on the Chinese side during the Korean War. The nickname of the vehicle was "Suka" meaning Bitch.

LEFT: **This SU-76 has been painted up in a disruptive winter pattern with whitewash. The large driver's hatch in the centre of the glacis is in the open position. The exhaust system was inadequate on this vehicle and resulted in some of the fumes entering the fighting compartment.**

SU-76 SPG

Country: USSR
Entered service: 1942
Crew: 4
Weight: 11,176kg/11 tons
Dimensions: Length – 5m/16ft 5in
    Height – 2.20m/7ft 3in
    Width – 2.74m/9ft
Armament: Main – 76.2mm/3in 1942 ZiS 3 gun
    Secondary – Small arms
Armour: Maximum – 35mm/1.38in
Powerplant: 2 x GAZ 6-cylinder 52.2kW/70hp petrol engine
Performance: Speed – 45kph/28mph
    Range – 450km/280 miles

LEFT: **The short barrel of the SU-122 is clearly seen along with the very large gun mantle. These vehicles were copied from the German StuG III but never had the same success.**
ABOVE: **An SU-100 vehicle which replaced most of the SU-122 and SU-85 vehicles in combat. One problem the SU-100 had was that it was not as manoeuvrable in narrow lanes or woods due to the long gun barrel.**

SU-122 Medium Self-Propelled Gun

This was the first self-propelled weapon to be mounted on the T-34 chassis and would lead the way to a whole family of guns based on this very famous tank.

The Soviet Army had been very impressed by the success of the German StuG vehicles, so in April 1942 the Main Artillery Directorate (GAU – *Glavniy Artilleriskoye Upravleniye)* issued a requirement for a self-propelled close-support gun. SPGs were a lot cheaper and quicker to produce than a tank mainly due to the tank's turret and turret-ring bearing race that were complicated to manufacture and required the use of specialist engineering equipment. Several vehicles were put forward by a

number of different design bureaux in consultation with the Commissariat for the Tank Industry (NKTP), but none of these passed the trials stage.

In October 1942 the State Defence Committee (GKO) ordered the design bureaux to have another look at an SPG design, but this time only using the T-34 chassis. The Uralmash plant in Sverdlovsk came up with the winning design. They removed the front and turret area of the T-34 chassis and mounted an all-welded box structure on the top of the opening. The glacis plate was made from one piece of sloped armour, and the sides of the fighting compartment were sloped as well. The new vehicle was designated the SU-35

and mounted the M-30 Model 1938 122mm/4.8in howitzer. On the successful completion of trials it was ordered into production in December 1942. GKO changed the name of the vehicle to SU-122 as it entered service in January 1943. Production finished in the summer of 1944, by which time 1,100 vehicles had been made.

It was intended to mix the SU-76 and the SU-122 in the same assault gun units, but due to the technical problems of the SU-76 this never worked. Each SU-122 regiment consisted of 16 vehicles divided into four batteries. These vehicles were slowly replaced by the SU-100, but some could still be found in service into the 1950s.

ABOVE: **The extended range fuel tanks on the rear of the vehicle can be seen, as well as the very short barrel length. A two-man tree saw is fitted as standard to the hull of the vehicle: this item was fitted to all Soviet armoured vehicles.**

SU-122 Medium SPG

Country: USSR
Entered service: 1943
Crew: 4
Weight: 30,480kg/30 tons
Dimensions: Length – 6.95m/22ft 10in
　　　　Height – 2.45m/8ft
　　　　Width – 3m/9ft 10in
Armament: Main – 122mm/4.8in M-30 howitzer
　　　　Secondary – 12.7mm/0.5in machine-gun
Armour: Maximum – 45mm/1.77in
Powerplant: V-2-34M 12-cylinder 375kW/500hp diesel engine
Performance: Speed – 55kph/34mph
　　　　Range – 271km/168 miles

Somua MCG Half-Track

LEFT: **This Somua has been fitted with an armoured roof on which an eight-tube Nebelwerfer rocket launcher has been mounted. One weakness of this vehicle was that the front wheels were very easily damaged.** ABOVE: **This U304 (f) half-track has been turned into an armoured ambulance by the Germans. The front of the vehicle is fitted with an unditching roller. This vehicle used the same chassis and track as the larger Somua.**

In the 1920s, the French led the world in the development of the half-track, especially using the Kegresse-type suspension. This system with its rubber tracks was even bought by the Germans and built under licence. In 1935, the Somua Company produced the MCG-type half-track, with production lasting until the invasion of France by the Germans in 1940. A year later they would produce an improved version, the MCL. In total 2,543 of both types of vehicle were built.

These vehicles were originally built for the French artillery as tractors for the 155mm/6.1in gun, and, using a heavy duty trailer, as general towing tractors for tank recovery. Most of these half-tracks were fitted with a jib with block and tackle for lifting the rear of the gun carriage up and on to the towing hook. They were not armoured and there was a standard wooden cargo bed behind the driver's cab.

The Germans captured over 2,000 of these vehicles and put them back into service with their own artillery units where they acted as tractors and supply vehicles. The MCL was redesignated the Le Zgkw S303 (f) while the MCG was given the designation of Le Zgkw S307 (f). In 1944, the Germans started to convert a number of these vehicles into self-propelled weapon carriers. All of these conversions were fitted with an armoured body and crew compartment, while 16 of them were converted into self-propelled anti-tank gun vehicles by the fitting of a

7.5cm/2.95in PaK40. Another conversion was the installation of sixteen 81mm/3.2in French mortars mounted in two rows of eight on the back of the half-track. The mortars would be preloaded and fired electrically from inside the armoured cab when the S307 had been driven to the desired position in the combat area. Other vehicles were fitted with various types of rocket launchers such as the Nebelwerfer.

These converted vehicles were issued to German units based in France, while some of the basic half-tracks remained in France and others were sent to Italy or the Eastern Front.

LEFT: **This Somua half-track has been converted to carry the German PaK40 AT gun. The gun and fighting compartment were placed at the rear of the vehicle. The driver's position was located in front of the gun.**

Somua MCG Half-Track

Country: France
Entered service: 1935
Crew: 3
Weight: 8,636kg/8.5 tons
Dimensions: Length – 5.3m/17ft 4in
　　　　Height – 1.95m/6ft 4in
　　　　Width – 1.88m/6ft 2in
Armament: Main – None
　　　　Secondary – Small arms
Armour: None
Powerplant: Somua 4-cylinder 45kW/60hp petrol engine
Performance: Speed – 36kph/22mph
　　　　Range – 170km/106 miles

LEFT AND BELOW: **This vehicle has been given the name of "Darlington" by its crew. The gun has been placed on a platform between the driver's and the brakeman's armoured cabins. The wheels for the gun have been stowed on the side of the vehicle, and the ammunition for the gun has been stored in the gap between the vehicle's brakeman's cabin and the engine compartment.**

The Gun Carrier

The Gun Carrier was a vehicle well ahead of its time and if it had been deployed more appropriately could have had a great impact on the outcome of World War I. These vehicles should have been able to take guns forward very quickly to help bolster the gains made by British infantry and help hold off the subsequent German counter-attack. They were ordered in October 1916 and were delivered to the army in France in July 1917.

The Gun Carrier used the engine and transmission of the Mk I tank, the basic vehicle being made up of six boxes. The tracks ran around two boxes 457mm/18in wide, 9.1m/30ft long and 1.5m/5ft high that made up the sides of the

vehicle. Above the tracks at the front of the vehicle were two one-man boxes; the one on the right was for the driver, the one on the left was for the brake man. Between the tracks was a platform open at one end while at the other was a box structure with a crew compartment, ammunition storage and the engine room. The open platform extended between the tracks and acted as a loading ramp which could be raised or lowered to mount a gun. A loading trolley which was housed on the platform could be run out in front of the vehicle and the gun would then be positioned over it. Its wheels were removed and the gun winched back on to the platform on the trolley. The wheels of the gun were then

placed on the side of the carrier. Guns such as the 152mm/5.98in howitzer could be fired from the carrier, making this vehicle the first true SPG.

These vehicles were first used at the Third Battle of Ypres in 1917, when they carried forward a number of 60pdr guns and several hundred tons of ammunition. They also carried out a limited number of night shoot missions on the German positions and some gas attacks. However, their main task was to carry supplies forward as each vehicle could do the work of 300 men. Well-suited to the conditions of the Western Front, they would remain in use as supply vehicles for the rest of the war.

ABOVE: **The large box structure at the rear of the vehicle housed the engine in the front and a crew compartment in the rear. At the rear of the carrier are the Mk I steering wheels.**

The Gun Carrier

Country: UK
Entered service: 1917
Crew: 4 plus gun crew
Weight: 34,544kg/34 tons
Dimensions: Length – 9.14m/30ft
   Height – 2.85m/9ft 4in
   Width – 2.49m/8ft 2in
Armament: Main – None
   Secondary – Small arms
Armour: Maximum – 8mm/0.315in
Powerplant: Daimler 6-cylinder 78kW/105hp petrol engine
Performance: Speed – 5.96kph/3.7mph
   Range – 56km/35 miles

LEFT: **The vehicle is fitted with four out-riggers and each one has a jack on it. The driver and vehicle commander's positions are very exposed as it that of the gun crew who also had to ride on the open back of the truck.** ABOVE: **The driver's position in the Thorneycroft. In front of the steering wheel is the fuel tank, while on the outside of the vehicle is the large hand brake and a rubber bulb horn. The gear selector is under the steering wheel.**

Thorneycroft "J" Type 13pdr Self-Propelled AA Gun

The Basingstoke firm of John Thorneycroft had a long history of producing trucks to meet a military standard. The design and development of the "J" Type 3-ton General Service truck started in 1912 and it was ready and in production for the Government Subsidy Trials that were held during 1913–14. The British government introduced a subsidy scheme that allowed private companies to buy lorries suitable for military service and, in return for a grant of 110 pounds towards the purchase price of the vehicle, to place

them at the disposal of the government in times of national emergency. The "J" Type won most of its classes in the trials and it was also the lightest vehicle in the 3-ton class. The British Army were supplied with 5,000 of these vehicles between 1914–18, and by the end of World War I it would be the most highly mechanized force in the world. These vehicles would remain in production until 1926 and stay in service with the British Army until 1930. They were also used in a number of specialist roles providing the chassis for variants such as mobile anti-aircraft guns and mobile field workshops.

At the start of the World War I, the British Army had no anti-aircraft guns. This led to a stopgap solution where guns were mounted on vehicles to provide a mobile defensive capacity. Thorneycroft built 183 of these vehicles between November 1915 and September 1916. The gun selected was the British

LEFT: **The armament for the vehicle was the QF (quick-firing) 13pdr 9cwt Mk 1. The pedestal was kept to a very basic design and was fitted with an 18pdr mounting for the gun. A number of these guns remained in service in Canada until 1930.**

13pdr, which was removed from its normal carriage and mounted on a high-angle pedestal on the rear of the vehicle to improve its elevation. The standard 13pdr munitions were not powerful enough to reach higher flying aircraft so the 13pdr shell was fitted to the 18pdr propellant cartridge. The new gun was called the 13pdr 9cwt anti-aircraft gun.

These vehicles were well-liked by their crews and were very reliable. They would see service on the Western Front until the end of the war even if they were originally intended as a stopgap weapon. The "J" Type did have one failing however and that was a very poor cross-country ability.

Thorneycroft "J" Type 13pdr SPAAG

Country: UK
Entered service: 1915
Crew: 8
Weight: 3,302kg /2.3 tons
Dimensions: Length – 6.7m/22ft 2in
   Height – 3.2m/10ft 5 in
   Width – 2.2m/7ft 2 in
Armament: Main – 5.9kg/13pdr, 457kg/9cwt
   Mk 1 AA gun
   Secondary – Small arms
Armour: None
Powerplant: Thorneycroft 4-cylinder, side valve, 30kW/40hp petrol engine
Performance: Speed – 27.4kph/14.5mph
   Range – 201km/125 miles

Troop Carrier/Supply Mk IX Tank

LEFT: **Next to the driver's visor is a ball-mounting for a machine-gun. The twin set of rails passing over the top of the vehicle is for an unditching beam that was carried by all British tanks.**
BELOW: **The screw-like device at the front of the track sponson is the track-tensioning device and was used to take up the slack in the track.**

The development of supply tanks was a major step towards the full mechanization of the British Army, these vehicles making their appearance in the summer of 1917. Two supply vehicles would appear at the same time: the Gun Carrier and a converted version of the Mk I gun tank, both having a large impact on the battlefield. In the case of the Mk I conversion, the gun sponsons were removed and replaced with 91cm/3ft mild steel sponsons that had a tendency to dig into the ground and slow the tank down. The handling was terrible on both vehicles. However, the significant issue was that these new vehicles could each free up 300 men from the job of moving supplies, and this meant that 300 trained infantry could be used in other roles. The next tank to be converted was the Mk IV gun tank and some 200 of these were freed up from combat duties for conversion into supply tanks.

The Mk IX was the first purposed built supply tank to be designed from scratch rather than being converted from a combat tank. Designed by Lieutenant G. J. Rackham in September 1917, it would enter service in France in October 1918, but only 35 of these vehicles were built by the end of the war. To give extra space in the vehicle, the engine was located in a position just behind the driver, and two machine-guns were fitted, one in the front beside the driver and the other in the rear. This vehicle was designed to carry 30 fully armed men across No Man's Land and into the German position, thus making it the first APC. The Mk IX could alternatively carry 10,160kg/10 tons of supplies, loading and unloading being carried out through four oval doors, two on each side of the vehicle and opposite to each other.

The load capacity of the vehicle was further increased by towing a specially designed sledge, which was developed by the tank workshop in France and allowed an additional 10,160kg/10 tons of supplies to be moved. Sadly, the Mk IX proved to be underpowered, slow, and very cumbersome to drive and handle.

RIGHT: **This vehicle has been painted in a standard World War I camouflage pattern. The large entrance and exit oval doors can be clearly seen. Opposite these on the other side of the vehicle were two more doors.**

Troop Carrier Mk IX	
Country: UK	
Entered service: 1918	
Crew: 4	
Weight: 37,592kg/37 tons	
Dimensions: Length – 9.70m/31ft 10in	
Height – 2.57m/8ft 5in	
Width – 2.46m/8ft 1in	
Armament: Main – 2 x Hotchkiss 8mm/0.315in	
machine-guns	
Secondary – None	
Armour: Maximum – 10mm/0.394in	
Powerplant: Ricardo 6-cylinder 112kW/150hp	
petrol engine	
Performance: Speed – 6kph/4mph	
Range – 193km/120 miles	

LEFT: **A Universal Carrier towing a 6pdr AT gun. The crew of the gun are perched on the top of the carrier as there is no room for them to sit inside. The carrier is also piled high with personal kit. The Germans captured a number of these and pressed them into service as Panzerjager Bren. This was just one amongst a wide variety of uses they made of them.**

Universal Carriers

The original role of an infantry carrier was as a fast, lightly armoured vehicle to transport a light machine-gun section into battle and to support an infantry section attack. Each infantry section would be issued with one carrier. By 1939 there were four different types of carrier in service with the British Army, but it was decided at this point that the cavalry carrier was no longer required and to simplify production by standardizing on one universal design for all purposes. The first production contract was issued in April 1939 and with a few modifications it would remain in production for the whole of World War II, with some 35,000 vehicles being produced in Britain alone.

The Universal Carrier No.1 Mk I was the first version to be placed into production and entered service in 1940. It had a riveted hull, which was made of armour plate and provided some protection for the bodies of the crew when sitting down, but none for their heads and shoulders. The engine, a Ford V8

48.5kW/65hp, had a large fan fitted to it to draw cooling air into the radiator and this made it extremely noisy. As it was mounted in the middle of the crew compartment, which was divided into two equal parts, conversation between the crew of the carrier was impossible. The driver was located on the right in the front of the carrier with the gunner, who manned the machine-gun, sitting next to him. Steering was controlled by a simple steering wheel that connected to the braking system on the tracks. When moved firmly left or right this would turn the vehicle sharply, but if it was only moved a few degrees the carrier used track-warp to turn the vehicle in a wide circle. This gave the carrier great manoeuvrability and good cross-country ability.

The Mk II had an improved engine, the Ford V8 63.4kW/85hp, and better stowage, while the Mk III was of all-welded construction and again had improvements to the engine and stowage.

ABOVE: **A Universal Carrier that has been converted into the amphibious flamethrower called the "Dragonfly". The flotation screen is in the folded-down position. When in the water, the screen comes above the height of the vehicle.**
RIGHT: **This Universal Carrier has got water in the engine and has stalled before reaching dry land. The vehicle is covered in personal equipment.**

LEFT: **This Universal Carrier has been issued to African troops in East Africa. The Carrier is armed with a single Boys AT rifle.** BELOW: **This Carrier has just landed in France on June 6, 1944. The vehicle is fitted with the deep-wading screens, which helped stop water entering the engine. The Carrier has equipment piled up in the rear.**

A large number of infantry sections would carry out field modifications to their carrier by fitting more and heavier machine-guns such as the 7.62mm/30cal or the 12.7mm/50cal. In some cases, until the supply of tanks had improved, the carrier would act as a substitute in the jungles of the Far East.

The Carrier Armoured Observation Post, No.1 Mk II, was one of many conversions of the Universal Carrier. The OP Carrier was fitted with cable drums for field telephones and a No.19 radio set. This vehicle carried a crew of four. The machine-gun aperture in the gunner's position was covered over and the Bren gun was mounted on a pintle in the rear. Some 5,400 of these vehicles were produced, mainly for the artillery. Other conversions included the mounting of the 2pdr anti-tank gun on some 200 Carrier chassis. This proved to be very successful and would remain in British service until 1946. The Carrier was also used to tow the 6pdr (57mm) anti-tank gun. In 1942, a special Universal Carrier was designed to carry a 76.2mm/3in mortar and its crew, along with 30 rounds of ammunition. These were mainly produced by the Wolseley Motor Company, who had built some 14,000 of this type of carrier by the end of World War II.

One of the most successful conversions of the Universal Carrier carried a flamethrower and was known as the Wasp. Production of these vehicles started in 1942 and an order for 1,000 of them was placed in September that year. The Wasp Mk I had two large fuel tanks for the flame gun fitted in the crew compartments. The pipe work then passed over the top of the vehicle and down into the gunner's position in the front of the vehicle. The Mk I was deemed unsuitable for action by 1943 and was replaced by the Wasp Mk II. This carried 273 litres/60 gallons of fuel for the flame gun and had a range of 91.4m/300ft.

The Universal Carrier was inevitably used in many roles for which it was never originally intended, and would carry a great diversity of weapons. It was to serve on all fronts with British and Commonwealth troops throughout World War II. The Germans captured a number of British carriers and pressed them into service, calling them "Panzerjager Bren".

RIGHT: **This Universal Carrier has been fitted with a Vickers machine-gun, and has a crew of four. The rear of the vehicle has extra jerry cans fitted to it, and canvas covers are rolled up and stored on the carrier.**

Universal Carrier No.1 Mk II

Country: UK
Entered service: 1942
Crew: 3
Weight: 4,064kg/4 tons
Dimensions: Length – 3.76m/12ft 4in
   Height – 1.63m/5ft 4in
   Width – 2.11m/6ft 11in
Armament: Main – Bren 7.7mm/0.303in
   light machine-gun
   Secondary – Small arms
Armour: Maximum – 12mm/0.47in
Powerplant: Ford V8 8-cylinder 63.4kW/85hp
   petrol engine
Performance: Speed – 52kph/32mph
   Range – 258km/160 miles

Wespe 10.5cm Self-Propelled Gun

LEFT: **This is an ammunition carrier for the Wespe, basically a Wespe without the gun. The driver's top hatch and front visor are in the fully open position. This particular vehicle has been captured from the Germans by the French Maquis.** ABOVE: **This is one of the prototype Wespe vehicles and is being finished off by a small team of men from the manufacturer, FAMO.** BELOW: **The engine is mounted under the gun, with the air intakes built into the side of the fighting compartment. The crew area at the rear of the vehicle is very small.**

When the Panzer II was withdrawn from front-line service in early 1942 and relegated to second-line duties, a number of these chassis were made available for conversion into SPG mounts. A design competition was run between the Panzer II, III and IV chassis to find a suitable mounting of the 10.5cm/ 4.13in le FH18/2 howitzer, and the Panzer II Alkett design was chosen.

The vehicle that won was the Wespe (Wasp) which was built on a modified Panzer II chassis. The first of these new vehicles were produced by Famo in March 1943 and entered service with the German Army in May 1943. The initial construction contract was for 1,000 vehicles but this was later reduced to 835, of which 150 were munitions carriers. The munitions carriers were the same specification as the gun vehicle except that the gun was not mounted; it could carry 90 rounds of ammunition. The Wespe had the main gun mounted in the rear of the vehicle in an open-topped fighting compartment. The

sides of this were made of 10mm/0.394in sloped armour and it had storage for 32 rounds of ammunition. The engine was placed in the middle of the vehicle, with the engine cooling-system louvers completely redesigned from the Panzer II and placed in the sides of the vehicle. The driver sat at the front in a separate compartment and the only contact he had with the rear of the vehicle was by intercom. The crew consisted of five men: the driver, commander, and three gun crew. The first versions of the Wespe were built on standard Panzer II chassis but this made the fighting compartment very small and cramped. The modified chassis was extended by 254mm/10in which resulted in an increased space between the road wheels and rear idler, but this did not improve the cramped conditions in the rear fighting compartment. The suspension system had to be strengthened to absorb the recoil of the gun, with bump-stop springs being added to the first, second and fifth road wheel. The production run was completed in August 1944 when it was intended to replace the vehicle with a Waffenträger (Weapon Carrier) with a turret-mounted 10.5cm/4.13in gun.

Several critical reports were written about the Wespe by the German units using it as it had several severe mechanical problems. The steering gear wore out very quickly in France and (especially) in Italy due to the narrow roads and tight turns. The brakes became covered in oil due to the leaking final drive, a fault that was never properly cured. It caused problems in convoy due to its slow speed and it did not cope well with the mud of the Russian spring and autumn, due to its narrow tracks which caused it to sink.

The combat debut for the Wespe was the great tank battle of Kursk, where it had been issued to six Panzer Divisions especially for the battle. The Wespe was intended to be deployed several miles behind the main action, rather than in the front line, but at Kursk this was not to be the case. However, due to its small size all but two of the Wespe managed to escape, having accounted for several Soviet tanks. Twelve Wespe were sent to the 17th Panzer Division on the Eastern Front where they fired off 18,000 rounds at the Soviet forces during the fighting around Orel and the withdrawal to the river Dnieper in August 1943. Another detachment of 12 Wespe vehicles was sent to Italy to join the 26th Panzer Division in November 1943, but in just four weeks none was left in service due to mechanical breakdowns. It had also been discovered that the vehicles could not be used in battery formations due to the nature of the Italian landscape and they were more often used on their own as single guns in the "shoot and scoot" role. It was therefore decided that the bulk of the Wespe production would be sent to the Eastern Front where its mechanical problems were not such a handicap.

The Wespe was disliked by its crews, as there was very little working space in the cramped crew compartment and nowhere for their personal kit. In addition, the vehicle was not reliable and there was no protection from the weather due to the low silhouette of the vehicle.

TOP: **This Wespe is taking part in the Battle of the Bulge in the winter of 1944. Ammunition has been laid out on the rear door of the vehicle to keep it clean, ready for a bombardment. The small size of the fighting compartment is very clear in this picture.** ABOVE: **This Wespe has had the muzzle brake removed from the end of the barrel. The air intakes for the engine can be seen between the two American soldiers. The driver's top hatch is in the open position.**

ABOVE: **The Panzer II chassis and running gear can be clearly seen, but the vehicle is missing its exhaust. This should be mounted on the lower rear hull of the Wespe.**

Wespe 10.5cm SPG

Country: Germany
Entered service: 1943
Crew: 5
Weight: 11,176kg/11 tons
Dimensions: Length – 4.82m/15ft 10in
　　Height – 2.31m/7ft 7in
　　Width – 2.28m/7ft 6in
Armament: Main – 10.5cm/4.13in le FH18 howitzer
　　Secondary – 7.92mm/0.312in MG34 machine-gun
Armour: Maximum – 30mm/1.18in
Powerplant: Maybach HL62TR 6-cylinder 104kW/140hp petrol engine
Performance: Speed – 40kph/25mph
　　Range – 140km/87 miles

Glossary

AA Anti-Aircraft.

AFV Armoured Fighting Vehicle.

AP Armour-Piercing.

APC Armoured Personnel Carrier.

APU Auxiliary Power Unit.

ARV Armoured Recovery Vehicle.

barbette An open-topped turret.

bustle Rear storage container on a vehicle (named after the "bustle", the bulge on the back of a lady's skirt in the early 20th century).

"buttoned up" All hatches are shut with the crew inside.

calibre Diameter of the bore of a gun barrel.

chain gun Machine-gun.

chassis Running gear of vehicles: axles, road wheels etc.

closed-down All hatches are shut.

coaxial The secondary armament mounted to fire alongside the main armament.

cupola Domed turret fitted with vision devices, frequently for use of vehicle commander.

double-baffle Muzzle brake with two holes.

glacis Defensive sloping front plate on an armoured vehicle.

GP General Purpose.

GPMG General Purpose Machine-Gun, typically 7.62mm/0.3in calibre.

HE High-Explosive.

HEAT High-Explosive Anti-Tank.

HMG Heavy Machine-Gun, typically 12.7mm/0.5in calibre.

hull The main body of the vehicle above the chassis.

LMG Light Machine-Gun, typically 7.62mm/0.3in calibre.

LVTP Landing Vehicle Tracked Personnel.

mantlet Protective covering for the hole in the turret where the main armament emerges.

muzzle brake Way of slowing down the recoil of the barrel by using the excess gases from the propellant charge.

November Parade Annual military parade in the USSR to celebrate the successful Communist Revolution in 1917.

pdr Contraction of "pounder" – old British measurement for artillery pieces, which were measured by weight of their shell, e.g. "6pdr" – six-pounder.

pistol ports An opening in a vehicle allowing small arms to be used from inside.

portee Vehicle transporter for an artillery piece.

prime mover Dedicated tractor unit, for example one whose first job is to shift guns.

pulpit Slang term for a raised gunner's or driver's position.

RNAS Royal Naval Air Service: the naval arm of the British military air forces between 1911 and 1918.

Russia (rather than USSR) The old Russian empire before the foundation of the Soviet Union in 1917. All vehicles from this region coming into service before 1917 are designated as being from Russia.

Sd Kfz German abbreviation for *Sonderkraftfahrzeug*: Special Purpose Motor Vehicles.

section vehicle Either a platoon commander's vehicle or a vehicle which can carry an infantry section of 10 men.

Soviet Union Colloquial name for the USSR.

spaced armour Armour built in two layers with a space in between.

SPG/H Self-Propelled Gun/ Howitzer.

standardized (of US vehicles) Term used when a vehicle is accepted into service with the US Army and given a military designation.

sustained rate of fire Rate of fire which a gun-crew can keep up over a period of time, not just for a short burst.

track grousers Attachments to tracks for extra grip over soft ground or ice.

uparmoured Increases in the original basic armour fitted to a vehicle.

USSR (rather than Russia) Union of Soviet Socialist Republics, founded in 1917 from the former Russian empire. All vehicles from this region coming into service after 1917 are designated as being from the USSR.

vision slits/slots An opening in a vehicle fitted with a vision device.

weapon station Weapons firing position.

White Russians Counter-revolutionaries in the civil war in the Soviet Union following the Revolution in 1917, opposing the Communist forces (the "Reds").

Index

Acknowledgements

The author would like to thank David Fletcher, historian at the Tank Museum, Bovington, and his staff, the DAS MT Section, Duxford, and the Cambridge Branch of MAFVA, for all their help and advice. A special thank you to Bridget Pollard for all her encouragement and help, especially "de-jargoning".

The publisher would like to thank the following for the use of their pictures in the book (l=left, r=right, t=top, b=bottom, m=middle). Every effort has been made to acknowledge the pictures properly; however, we apologize if there are any unintentional omissions, which will be corrected in future editions.

After the Battle: 55tl.

Imperial War Museum Photographic Archive: 8–9 (AP 61131); 11br (Q 72834); 13tl (Q 51506); 13m (HU 89293); 13b (Q 26825); 15tl (KID 51); 20tl (MA 6636); 20b (NXF 21959); 21tl (AP 61131); 21tr (NYF 18777); 21m (BU 3398); 21b (BU 4782); 22m (E 16517); 23umr (BU 4784); 23lmr (HU 91730); 26–7 (K 685); 31tl (Q 7036); 32tr (STT 3222); 40tl (NA 5076); 40tr (NA 7259); 40b (NA 6815); 41tl (NA 15906); 42b; 43m (B 11628); 43b (IMD 4127); 44t (K 685); 44m (O 131); 44b (O 97); 45tl (BU 3341); 45tr (BU 2845); 45b (B 6011); 47t (E 21333); 48b (E 18530); 49tl (HU 87652); 50; 54tl (H 38157); 54b (NA 8429); 58tl (B 11921); 58m (NA 675); 58b (B 5205); 59tl (E 21338); 59tr (EA 56553); 59b (EA 56506); 60b (BU 1389); 64tl

(B 6045); 65t (E 16522); 65m (E 16553); 65b (E 16519); 68m (BU 9267); 72b (NA 15330); 73tr (B 5413); 74 (DXP85/34/1); 77tr (NA 120); 78b (NA 15506); 79tl (NA 1960); 79tr (STT 4601); 79b (NA 15570); 80tl (MH 9046); 81b (Q 2957); 83b (MH 3755); 88t (E 18869); 88b (NA 6265); 89tl (NA 15051); 89b (B 5032); 91b (NA 15165); 92tl (Q 90301); 92br (E 378); 93b (Q 1222); 94t (E 7209); 94m (FLM 394); 95t (MH 9044); 96t (NA 4664); 96m (HU 75844); 96b (B 13254); 102b (B 13737); 104t (NA 7750); 104bl (MH 6107); 104br (MH 10084); 107t (B 9807); 111tr (HU 54177); 111m (NA 15178); 111b (PC 399); 122t (NA 4199); 122br (NA 4184); 123tl (K 7806); 123tr (B 5023).

Jack Livesey Collection: 3; 19tr; 19br; 22t; 38b; 42t; 47m;

47b; 49tr; 49b; 55b; 57; 60tl; 60tr; 64tr; 64b; 66; 67t; 67um; 68t; 68b; 69–70; 71ml; 75; 76; 78t; 80b; 83tl; 83tr; 84; 88m; 89tr; 102tr; 106; 107b; 110; 111tl; 115tl; 117tr; 120.

Tank Museum Photographic Archive: 1; 2; 6; 7; 10; 11tr; 11mr; 11ml; 12; 13tr; 14; 15tr; 15m; 15br; 16–18; 19tl; 19ml; 19mr; 23t; 24–5; 28–30; 31tr; 31b; 32tl; 32b; 33–7; 38t; 39; 41tr; 41mr; 46; 48tl; 48tr; 51–3; 54tr; 55tr; 56; 61–3; 71t; 71b; 72tl; 72tr; 73tl; 73b; 77tl; 77b; 80tr; 81tl; 81tr; 82; 85–7; 90; 91tl; 91tr; 92tr; 92bl; 93t; 94b; 95b; 97–101; 105; 108–9; 112–14; 115tr; 115b; 116; 117tl; 117b; 118–19; 121; 122bl; 123b; 124–5; 128.

TRH Pictures: 67lm; 67b; 103b.

Victory Memorial Museum: 5t; 23b; 102tl; 103t; 103m; 126; 127.